Facilitation Skills
TRAINING

Donald V. McCain and
Deborah Davis Tobey

ASTD
PRESS

Alexandria, Virginia

ASTD Press is an internationally renowned source of insightful and practical information on workplace learning and performance topics, including training basics, evaluation and return-on-investment (ROI), instructional systems development (ISD), e-learning, leadership, and career development.

Ordering information: Books published by ASTD Press can be purchased by visiting our website at store.astd.org or by calling 800.628.2783 or 703.683.8100.

Library of Congress Control Number: 2007 921 480

ISBN-10: 1-56286-474-2
ISBN-13: 978-1-56286-474-3

ASTD Press Editorial Staff
Director: Cat Russo
Manager, Acquisitions & Author Relations: Mark Morrow
Editorial Manager: Jacqueline Edlund-Braun
Editorial Assistant: Kelly Norris
Copyeditors: Kathy L. Hahn and Christine Cotting
Proofreader: Kris Patenaude
Indexer: April Michelle Davis
Interior Design and Production: UpperCase Publication Services, Ltd.
Cover Design: Steve Fife
Cover Illustrator: Todd Davidson

Printed by Victor Graphics, Inc., Baltimore, Maryland, www.victorgraphics.com.

The ASTD Trainer's WorkShop Series is designed to be a practical, hands-on road map to help you quickly develop training in key business areas. Each book in the series offers all the exercises, handouts, assessments, structured experiences, and ready-to-use presentations needed to develop effective training sessions. In addition to easy-to-use icons, each book in the series includes a companion CD-ROM with PowerPoint presentations and electronic copies of all supporting material featured in the book.

Other books in the Trainer's WorkShop Series:

- ◆ *New Supervisor Training*
  John E. Jones and Chris W. Chen

- ◆ *Customer Service Training*
  Maxine Kamin

- ◆ *New Employee Orientation Training*
  Karen Lawson

- ◆ *Leading Change Training*
  Jeffrey Russell and Linda Russell

- ◆ *Leadership Training*
  Lou Russell

- ◆ *Coaching Training*
  Chris W. Chen

- ◆ *Project Management Training*
  Bill Shackelford

- ◆ *Innovation Training*
  Ruth Ann Hattori and Joyce Wycoff

- ◆ *Sales Training*
  Jim Mikula

- ◆ *Communication Skills Training*
  Maureen Orey and Jenni Prisk

- ◆ *Strategic Planning Training*
  Jeffrey Russell and Linda Russell

- ◆ *Diversity Training*
  Cris Wildermuth, with Susan Gray

- ◆ *Teamwork Training*
  Sharon Boller

Contents

Facilitation of learning is not the same as making a presentation. The word *facilitate* comes from the Latin *facilis,* and means, "to make easy" (Bentley 1994). As learning facilitators, our job is to guide the learning process for our learners—in other words, to make their learning easy. Doing this effectively is an acquired skill.

We've written this book for you—the person who wants to teach others to enhance their learning facilitation skills. You might be working in human resource development within an organization, or you might be an employee of a company that provides facilitation skills training or train-the-trainer courses to organizational clients. Your learners may include subject matter experts who occasionally function in a training role or who are moving into a training role in their jobs, trainers who are ready to move beyond presenting information and using learning activities for their "fun" value only, faculty members in educational institutions who want to add skill and application to their classroom experiences, HR professionals or managers who contract with learning facilitators and want to evaluate their performance, and trainers whose organizations are holding the training function accountable for learners' performance back on the job.

The perspective of *Facilitation Training* is that facilitating learning experiences is about the learners—their growth and development, and their success. This book will help you teach others the knowledge and skills to shift the focus from the presenter to the learner.

For those of us whose background is in presentations and in content expertise, this learner-centric focus is a new paradigm. Many of us are used to focusing on ourselves and our preparedness for questions, our control of the group, and our expertise. *Facilitation Training* will enable you to provide your learners the skills to go beyond this standpoint to facilitate learning through focusing on the environment for learning, preparation, selection and use of media, and the use of learning and instructional strategies.

Facilitation of learning is both a skill and an art that finds its reward in others. A skilled facilitator reaps the reward from the learners: their success when they learn content, use and apply it, grow, and ultimately perform better back on the job.

A successful learning experience requires a good design, applicable content, and great facilitation. The goal of *Facilitation Training* is to provide a training course that will help you ultimately enhance the facilitation skills of training professionals. You'll be able to address critical areas in facilitation, including principles of adult learning, learner preferences, facilitator competencies and roles, use of learning activities and facilitation techniques, use of media, and assessment of the quality of your facilitation. Additional features include structuring the learning environment and handling "difficult" participants. This practical, ready-to-use program will enable you to quickly provide a high-quality, practical facilitation skills training course for your organization or client.

Our purpose in this book is to assist you in your training of facilitators while enhancing your facilitation skills. When you continue your learning journey by improving your own skills and those of others, you increase the learning that takes place in your classes, increase the probability of skill transfer back to your learners' jobs, and ultimately increase the impact of training on the organization.

We would like to dedicate this book to our spouses and families who provided support through this endeavor. We also want to thank so many of our peers who spoke with us and gave us feedback.

Donald McCain and Deborah Davis Tobey
August 2007

How to Use This Book Effectively: Introduction and Overview

What's in This Chapter?

- Discussion of and criteria for facilitator selection

- Explanation of a train-the-trainer process

- Basic assumptions regarding the material presented here

- Explanation of how to use this workbook most effectively

Facilitator Selection

Selecting quality facilitators helps ensure a quality learning experience. You may find yourself in a position where you need to select facilitators to lead a learning experience. In some cases, you may need to make a trade-off between facilitation skills and subject matter knowledge. This discussion will help you use more objective criteria to support your facilitator selection process.

The ingredients of quality facilitation are subject matter expertise, excellent presentation skills, and learning facilitation skills. A facilitator's credibility begins with subject matter expertise. For that reason, many organizations elect to have subject matter experts (SMEs) become trained facilitators of specific content areas.

SME facilitators need to be selected based on objective criteria. Some of these factors include

- knowledge of the industry and subject

- recognition, reputation, and acceptance within the organization

- years of experience in a particular job function or organizational role

- educational level

- availability to deliver the training consistently and according to schedule

- industry recognition

- good presentation skills (physical bearing, comfort in front of a group, voice quality)

- good learning facilitation skills.

Over and above these qualifications, a facilitator should posses certain behavioral competencies. The possession and use of these competencies will help ensure excellence in facilitation.

Train-the-Trainer

Facilitators selected to teach a specific training course should already possess learning facilitation skills. If they don't possess these skills, they're probably going to be participants in a facilitation training course like the one you're learning about in this book. Such a course will help them understand adult learning principles, use multiple sources of media, engage the participants, implement learning strategies, and assess knowledge and skill demonstration. Facilitation training courses are hands-on, practical, high-energy experiences tied to identified facilitation competencies. Additionally, because the design of a good facilitation training workshop is performance based, the participants will be required to demonstrate both knowledge and skill proficiency—an element you'll see in this course in a section on preparation for skill practice back on the job.

If you're responsible for the training function within an organization, or if you work with such organizations, you may be responsible for the train-the-trainer (T3) process related to specific training courses, in addition to the facilitation skills training discussed in this book. If that's the case, the following discussion is offered to assist you.

Once facilitators possess the required learning facilitation skills, they still need to participate in a specific T3 course for the learning experience they'll deliver. For example, a facilitator scheduled to facilitate a course on time management in his or her organization might take your facilitation skills training course, and would take a T3 to learn to teach the specific time management content.

The T3 session trains identified facilitators on the content, use of assessments, learning strategies, and so on as a total learning experience specific to that subject and that course. At this time, the facilitator gains an in-depth understanding of the specific course content, the flow of the learning experience, and the interrelationship of all the design elements. Each content area and how it should be taught will be discussed. The facilitator will practice delivering the learning experience, section by section, and getting direct feedback and coaching.

For any existing course, the new facilitator's T3 experience should include the following steps:

1. Participate in the T3 session.

2. Study the leader's guide to ensure knowledge of the content and the interrelationship of the leader's guide with the participant learning materials and media.

3. Participate as a learner for the entire program, making notes on areas of comfort or discomfort, questions regarding facilitator and participant interactions, positioning and response to content, learning strategies and assessments, completeness of the debriefing of learning strategies, and relevancy to the participants' jobs.

4. Co-lead sections of the course with an experienced facilitator and receive that person's specific feedback and coaching. This step may require several opportunities to co-lead so the facilitator-in-training will have an opportunity to become familiar with all aspects of the learning experience.

5. Make the content and examples her or his own. New facilitators will need to personalize some areas of the learning content, providing examples from their own experiences.

6. Deliver the learning experience as the primary facilitator with a trained facilitator observing and providing feedback and coaching. (There may need to be multiple deliveries following this format.)

7. Deliver the learning experience on an ongoing basis.

The T3 process results in the facilitator's ability to demonstrate the following:

- open and close the learning experience

- use the leader's guide and integrate it with the participant materials and media

- effectively facilitate discussions, exercises, and assessments

- use listening skills

- provide participant feedback

- ask and field questions

- build rapport with and understand the audience

- maintain participant interest

- incorporate adult learning principles

- create and maintain a supportive learning environment

- deal with difficult situations

- effectively use multiple forms of media

- evaluate knowledge and skills.

Ideally, facilitators are selected at the beginning of the design and development process for a specific training course. When facilitators are identified prior to that process, they should attend the various meetings with the client organization during which learning objectives, content, media, assessment instruments and process, and learning strategies are discussed. The potential facilitators should attend the pilot session. This begins the "ownership" process whereby the facilitators become immersed in the content as well as the intent of the learning experience.

If this is a new learning experience without previous facilitators to learn from, the new facilitator will deliver the learning experience to a pilot audience. A trained facilitator and SME will observe the facilitation and provide direct feedback and coaching. Pilot participants also will provide feedback through an extensive evaluation.

Using the feedback and coaching, the facilitator will then deliver the learning experience to the target audience. Again, a trained facilitator should be present to observe and provide feedback and coaching. The course evaluation information can supply participant feedback on the facilitator's skills; this is an ongoing process of delivery and feedback.

Working Assumption

We've focused *Facilitation Training* on the knowledge and skills required to become a great learning facilitator. Therefore, we must begin with the assumption that you already possess "platform" skills—comfort in front of a group, good presentation techniques (including stance, voice, gestures, and eye contact), and basic media savvy. We'll review and build on those skills in this book.

How to Use This Workbook and Accompanying CD Most Effectively

You'll find this book a useful resource for designing, developing, and facilitating workshops in teaching others to be excellent facilitators. You'll be able to custom design the skill-building facilitation training programs you need to present to audiences ranging from new facilitators to more seasoned facilitators who want to refresh their skills.

To benefit most from this book and the accompanying CD, we recommend that you follow these steps as you design your training program:

1. Skim the book. Quickly read through its entire contents. Study the "What's in This Chapter?" list at the front of each chapter. Get a good sense of the layout and structure of what's included in each chapter and in the overall book. Also, review the contents of the CD.

2. Become more familiar with various aspects of adult learning, your role as a facilitator, facilitation competencies and principles, and methods of personalizing the material.

3. Explore the basics of the learning activities. Chapter 3 presents a comprehensive agenda and is your guide for facilitating the two-day Advanced Facilitation Training course. The chapter presents ideas for creating the climate, planning and implementing learning activities, monitoring and providing feedback on those learning activities, as well as managing the schedule, and coping with difficult people. As you'll see, *Facilitation Training* is designed to help bring about learning. In some cases, there will be models and tools that can actually be used as part of facilitation training. We believe that you'll find

chapter 3 useful even if you're an experienced facilitator. It offers a review of good teaching practices and likely reinforces what you're already doing.

We recommend the two-day course as a complete experience for your learners because it provides a comprehensive training program. However, time constraints might dictate the use of a more compact workshop. If you want a shorter version of the course that still provides a wealth of knowledge and application of facilitation skills for the job, review chapter 4. There you'll find the comprehensive agenda and facilitator's guide for leading a one-day Facilitation Skills Training workshop with a focus on the facilitation of learning activities.

4. Chapters 5 and 6 support your facilitation training workshops. There you'll find all the learning activities, assessments, checklists, and worksheets to conduct a successful facilitation training program. Draw on these materials to support your delivery to potential facilitators.

All of the handouts and Microsoft PowerPoint slides referred to in the modules are included in the text and on the accompanying CD-ROM. Follow the instructions in Appendix C: Using the Compact Disc, and the CD document titled "How to Use This CD.doc" to access the various electronic documents.

The training materials in this book and on the CD include

- ◆ two-day and one-day training workshops that can be used as is or modified in response to the organization's needs, learning needs, or your own style

- ◆ activities that encourage active learning, integration of content, and strengthened learning application back on the job

- ◆ printable handouts designed to align with the training modules

- ◆ Microsoft PowerPoint presentations for use in guiding participants' learning and in focusing their energy.

Icons

For easy reference, icons are included in the margins throughout this workbook to help you quickly locate key elements in training design and instruction. These icons are described below.

CD: refers to materials included on the CD accompanying this workbook.

Clock: indicates recommended timeframes for specific activities.

Debrief: indicates a special type of guided discussion (see below for the description of a guided discussion) in which learners analyze the experience of a learning activity and in which learning points are reinforced.

Interactive Lecture: points out where the facilitator presents content, intersperses the content with questions to gain learner participation, and accepts and answers questions. (This differs from the traditional lecture because there is interaction and participation by the learners.)

Guided Discussion: denotes a planned discussion in which the facilitator prepares questions that will guide learners into discovery of the learning points.

Handouts: indicates materials that can be printed or copied to support training activities.

Key Point: alerts you to items that should be emphasized to participants or that are particularly salient for you as the facilitator.

Learning Activity: points out an exercise in which learners work with each other (or, on occasion, first alone and then with each other) on an assignment such as a self-assessment, discussion, game, case study, or role play. The facilitator participates as a monitor of the activity.

PowerPoint Slide: indicates PowerPoint presentations and individual slides.

What to Do Next: highlights recommend actions that you can take to transition from one section of this workbook to the next, or from a specific training activity to another within a training module.

What to Do Next

Reflect on your own experience with facilitation in your current or former organization. Take some time to answer the following questions: How effective was the facilitation? How did the participants respond to you and engage with the material and with other participants? What did the feedback reveal about your facilitation skills?

◆ ◆ ◆

We recognize that learners need to take the lead according to their abilities; not every participant starts at the same point. The next chapter discusses principles of adult learning, their implications for facilitating learning experiences, and the diverse learning styles you're likely to encounter among the participants in your workshops.

Facilitation Overview

- Discussion of adult learning principles

- Explanation of the role of a facilitator

- Identification of facilitator skills and competencies

- Discussion of the principles underlying the facilitation of learning

- Ways to personalize the material

Principles of Adult Learning

According to Nadler and Nadler (1994), "Learning is the acquisition of new skills, attitudes, and knowledge." Learning results in change. For facilitation effectiveness, the emphasis must be on both the acquisition and use of the new knowledge, skills, attitudes, and abilities. Through facilitation, we bring together adults and learning to help educate through self-discovery. This involves techniques for learners to learn from each other in the sharing of knowledge and experiences.

Mitchell (1998) indicates that there are basic principles of adult education, providing a framework for development and facilitation.

READINESS TO LEARN

Without learner readiness, there's resistance, and learning doesn't take place. The facilitator should encourage the participant to discuss his or her resistance openly. Once the nature of the resistance is understood, it can be addressed.

ACTIVE INVOLVEMENT IN LEARNING

Adults learn best when they are active participants in the learning process rather than passive recipients. People learn by doing. Allow participants to practice the skills being taught; maximize the time spent in practice and application through role play, case studies, demonstration and practice, participant presentations, and so forth (Mitchell 1998).

SELF-DIRECTED LEARNING

Adult learners are responsible for their own learning and are capable of self-direction. The facilitator must engage the learners in a process of inquiry and decision making and not just give information or knowledge to them.

TRIAL AND ERROR

Making mistakes is another way adults learn. According to Mitchell (1998), success motivates adults and makes them want to learn more, but they tend to remember mistakes and want to know how to correct them. As a facilitator, allow participants to make mistakes and to learn from them. Create a safe environment for trial and error while ensuring that the successes are reinforced and the learners capture those lessons learned.

BUILDING ON EXPERIENCE

Adults learn by connecting new information with what they already know (Mitchell 1998), moving from the known to the unknown. Some techniques to understand the audience's knowledge and experience include pretests, icebreakers (exercises or activities that bring everyone to a common understanding), participant profiles, and soliciting pre-course information by having participants respond to the course objectives.

SENSORY LEARNING

Although adult learners use all their senses (sight, hearing, touch, smell, and taste), individuals usually have a dominant or preferred sense on which they rely for learning new things (Mitchell 1998). Facilitation usually addresses the senses of sight (visual learning), hearing (auditory learning), and touch (kinesthetic learning).

Visual learners must see what they're learning—for example, via graphics, printed materials, PowerPoint slides, posters, and such. Auditory learners must interact with and apply content through listening and speaking—for instance, via discussions, oral presentations, music, acronyms, and so on. Kinesthetic learners interact with and apply content in a physical way. That need can be met through hands-on practice, such as taking notes, drawing pictures, building objects, and creating flipcharts.

LESS IS MORE

Effective facilitators take complex or new material and organize it in a simple way so participants can easily understand and apply the new information and skills. To manage the amount of material, content should directly align with specific learning objectives; content that doesn't fit those objectives should not be included. This allows time for skill practice and reinforcement.

BUILDING ON THEORY

Helping participants understand why the learning is important and putting it in context make the learning easier. Adults want theory presented in the context of applicability to the job and to real-life situations. Facilitators need to make clear the course's relevance to the learners' situations. They must be able to link the course objectives and content to the adult learners' need to know.

PRACTICE

Adults want to learn things that will help them solve a problem, do a task, or prepare for a position. Therefore, a key learning ingredient is practice, which not only increases proficiency but also increases the probability of retention.

"FIRST CRACK"

Training must be facilitated so that learners can get "first crack" at discovering the content as much as possible. If they know at least something about the content, then a discussion or activity is appropriate—not a lecture during which they remain passive.

FEEDBACK

Adults want and need feedback. Facilitators can give it through knowledge testing, skill practice checklists, role play, and case studies. Peer learners and you as facilitator can provide feedback on participants' comments as they are made or during debriefing activities.

INDIVIDUAL DIFFERENCES

Every participant brings a unique background, perspective, and set of personal biases, and each one learns differently. In addition, every adult learns at his or her own pace. Your job is to bring the slow learners along while challenging the fast learners.

Individual differences become greater with age and experience, including differences in learning style, time and place of learning, and depth of knowledge and expertise. Facilitators must accommodate different learning styles and depth of knowledge.

Roles of the Facilitator

A facilitator has many roles, discussed below—each supporting the overall goal of learning. As a facilitator fulfills these roles, she or he is also in charge of both the task (learning and applying knowledge and skills) and the process (how the learning and application happen) of conducting learning experiences. Each of the following roles focuses on managing a task or process.

LEADER OF THE GROUP

As leader, you create and sustain the environment for learning. You want participants interacting with you and other learners with the goal of acquiring new knowledge and skills. Your role is to help participants learn and apply the new knowledge and skills to their jobs. Managing the task and process as the leader involves

- ◆ encouraging group cohesiveness and direction. This can be accomplished by managing the group involvement process, ensuring group members are treated as equals, and encouraging group discussion.

- ◆ helping team members be sensitive to other members, involve all members, and establish and maintain group norms.

- ◆ providing feedback on participants' comments and individual and group activities. Give complete, honest, and balanced feedback.

MANAGER OF THE AGENDA

Maintaining the agenda is a task-focused facilitator role. Starting on time and staying on time may be difficult, but it's important in order to complete all the content and fully experience the learning strategies.

Once you get behind, you must make up time without sacrificing the quality of the learning experience. You must manage the time related to content, learning activities with debriefing sessions, action planning, and assessments. Although you may be able to negotiate extra time at the end of the day or have a working lunch, there's still the expectation of stopping on time.

ROLE MODEL FOR POSITIVE BEHAVIORS

Good facilitators model the behavior they're teaching. For example, if you're teaching facilitation skills, model the skills and behavior of an exemplary facilitator. As the facilitator of learning, you must always maintain a positive and professional demeanor. Seek positive solutions to constructive conflict; try to see the other's point of view.

CONTENT EXPERT

Being an expert in your content is part of the task focus. Participants expect you to speak beyond the generic script of your leader guide and make the content relevant to them. You can do that by asking and answering questions that take people deeper into the content, by sharing relevant experiences, and by using your learners' jargon. In essence, you want to demonstrate mastery of the subject in both content and application to the job.

There might be occasions when part of establishing your credibility as a content expert or as a facilitator involves letting the learners know what qualifies you to be in front of them. In these cases, produce a biography that outlines your background and experience, and place it in the front of their materials so they can read it at their leisure. Nothing takes the focus off the learners more quickly than the facilitator droning on about himself or herself at the beginning of the program!

CONSULTANT

As a consultant, adviser, or coach, you help the participants make sense of the concepts and apply them to their jobs within the context of their environment. This is the task part of learning—helping participants see the implications of new knowledge and skills for their own performance, their team's performance, and the performance of their business unit.

As a consultant, you may do some follow-up work to see the extent that the new knowledge and skills have transferred to the job. You can then identify enablers and barriers to knowledge and skill transfer, and help management address the situation.

Facilitator Competencies

Your effectiveness as a facilitator relies on your knowledge, skills, and individual characteristics or behavioral competencies. It's not enough to be an SME, or simply to make a good presentation. Expert facilitators have a full complement of competencies, and these are grouped by major category—knowledge, skills, and behaviors.

KNOWLEDGE COMPETENCIES

Knowledge, as it relates to facilitator competencies, is the organized body of things known about facilitating learning experiences. This includes facts, assumptions, concepts, principles, procedures, and/or processes:

- the organization's strategies, objectives, markets, customers, competitors, products or services, and so on

- adult learning principles

- learning theory

- needs assessment processes and needs assessmentresults for the specific seminar/workshop to be facilitated

- organizational, job, and individual performance indicators

- instructional design and development

- diversity awareness related to participant differences in learning

- methods and tactics to get organizational buy-in and support for learning

- group dynamics

- tactics for coaching and feedback

- training evaluation.

SKILLS COMPETENCIES

Facilitators exhibit skills competencies by actual demonstrations of the skill, which are measured by observation of the skill process or evaluation of the outcome (that is, product). Facilitation skills include

- verbal communication

- nonverbal communication, such as body posture, gestures, and facial expressions

- thinking in terms of systems, so as to see interrelationships among participants' input by recognizing the connecting patterns

- planning learning activities

- operating the equipment used in training

- writing on flipcharts for preparing standard charts and recording participants' comments

- listening actively and effectively

- summarizing and paraphrasing participant input

- providing coaching and feedback.

INDIVIDUAL CHARACTERISTICS OR BEHAVIORAL COMPETENCIES

People demonstrate individual characteristics by how they behave in given situations. Exhibit 2–1 is an extensive list and brief description of these behavioral competencies. There are 14 characteristic categories, each containing multiple behaviors.

The more competencies a facilitator possesses and the more effectively he or she uses those competencies, the better the performance, which directly affects the quality of the learning experience.

Principles Underlying Facilitation of Learning Experiences

There are 11 basic principles that will enhance the learning experience:

1. Facilitated learning is learner centered, not facilitator centered.

2. The facilitator is in the learning experience with the learners, not just an observer.

3. The facilitator's goal is to make learning happen.

4. Adult learners have specific needs that facilitators must fulfill for learning to occur.

Exhibit 2–1
Facilitator Behavioral Competencies

CHARACTERISTIC GROUPING	BEHAVIORAL COMPETENCIES
Initiative	1. Positions the learning experience with participants by building relationships and setting the climate 2. Positions the learning experience with participants to support the organization's strategies and objectives 3. Makes extra efforts to ensure participant learning and application of that learning on the job by focusing questions, examples, and plans on real-world examples 4. Takes self-directed action to remove learning and transfer barriers to achieve learning outcomes effectively and efficiently
Concern for continuous improvement	1. Uses adult learning principles to ensure learning 2. Monitors ongoing participant learning by soliciting feedback and analyzing performance on assessments 3. Plans and monitors facilitation to ensure efficient and effective use of time and greatest impact on learning
Customer service	1. Acts as a learning consultant to participants 2. Implements instructional strategies relative to participant needs 3. Builds networks among participants to support classroom learning and transfer to the job
Interpersonal understanding	1. Demonstrates and acts on an understanding of the collective concerns of the participants 2. Demonstrates and acts on an understanding of participants' personal interests, concerns, and motivations 3. Seeks to understand the motivations behind participants' behavior
Leading others	1. Promotes a spirit of cooperation among participants 2. Clarifies and communicates roles and expectations of facilitator and participants 3. Solicits the input of participants and leverages participant expertise through establishing collaborative relationships 4. Creates learner synergy through involvement in course instructional strategies

Exhibit 2–1, continued

Facilitator Behavioral Competencies

CHARACTERISTIC GROUPING	BEHAVIORAL COMPETENCIES
	5. Recognizes and rewards the contribution of participants
Developing others	**1.** Creates a learning environment that fosters learning and transfer **2.** Identifies job-related applications to course content **3.** Contributes to individual, team, and corporate knowledge **4.** Models development to support continuous learning **5.** Provides coaching to enhance learning
Analytical/problem solving	**1.** Implements a structured process of collecting course information and feedback **2.** Gathers the relevant information and takes action to resolve a problem or issue within the learning experience
Creativity and innovation	**1.** Uncovers opportunities for application of learning **2.** Takes innovative action to maximize the effectiveness of a learning experience **3.** Implements creative instructional strategies
Change management	**1.** Proactively recognizes situations where change in classroom learning is needed and initiates appropriate action **2.** Changes plans and acts in response to changing conditions or participant needs, rather than pursuing a single course of action **3.** Ensures that the participants embrace the need for the new knowledge, skills, and abilities (KSAs) taught in the learning experience
Risk taking	**1.** Takes appropriate risks to see new ideas, content, and instructional strategies accepted and/or implemented **2.** Supports participants who take appropriate risks
Communicating effectively	**1.** Makes effective verbal presentations (includes changing language or terminology to fit audience characteristics)

continued on next page

Exhibit 2–1, continued
Facilitator Behavioral Competencies

CHARACTERISTIC GROUPING	BEHAVIORAL COMPETENCIES
	2. Reads and understands verbal and nonverbal behavior and responds appropriately 3. Effectively uses nonverbal communication techniques
Influencing	1. Facilitates in a way that influences the participants to accept and use the new KSAs 2. Uses interpersonal and communication skills to gain acceptance of and commitment to course content and learning objectives 3. Gains commitment of participants by positioning the learning in terms of benefits meaningful to the participants 4. Builds trust between facilitator and participants, and among participants 5. Gains the cooperation and support of the participants
Organizational awareness	1. Expresses the benefits and disadvantages of participants' input using their business terminology 2. Acts as a catalyst for participants and their respective business units to improve performance through the use of the acquired KSAs 3. Recognizes and responds to organizational issues as they relate to the course content 4. Thinks organizationally and presents learning applications that address participants' jobs and organizational needs 5. Demonstrates an understanding of the organization's strategies, objectives, markets, products/services, informal political network
Personal effectiveness characteristics	1. Accurately and completely represents the training organization to participants 2. Serves as a role model for others regarding appropriate business conduct and ethical principles 3. Keeps emotions under control when facing adversity 4. Interacts effectively with varying levels of participants with different backgrounds and perspectives

5. Facilitators create opportunities for learners to share their own experiences and expertise.

6. In a learning event, all participants are sources for learning.

7. Facilitators protect and affirm ideas.

8. Facilitators are not entertainers. The facilitator's job is to be interested, not interesting.

9. Facilitators encourage and support balanced participation in the learning group.

10. Facilitators create a comfortable and supportive environment in which learners can take risks.

11. Facilitators remove obstacles from the learning process.

Making It Your Own: Personalizing the Material

Experienced facilitators personalize the course and materials to reflect their expertise and facilitation style. The more the materials fit you, and the more comfortable you are, the more conducive the climate is to learning.

YOUR MATERIALS

One aspect of personalization is simply reviewing the materials and becoming familiar with the flow. Identify the content you think is most critical and plan how you'll emphasize it and relate it to your learners' jobs. Identify content areas that you want to expand on. Think about and prepare for the most likely learner questions and comments.

EXAMPLES AND STORIES

Prepare examples and "war stories" from your own experiences that will illustrate content points. Practice telling these stories so that you're prepared to emphasize the points that best illustrate the content and application to participants' jobs. Be sure not to wing it when it comes to your stories and examples. Plan ahead; make sure the stories and examples are in alignment with the learning objectives, and rehearse them so that they flow smoothly.

HUMOR

Appropriate jokes and funny stories can be very effective in making a point and in establishing a comfortable climate. The following are some tips for using humor, jokes, and funny stories:

- ◆ The humorous item must be relevant to the learning and content at hand.

- ◆ Practice telling it so you know what to emphasize or exaggerate— and so you don't forget the punch line.

- ◆ Make sure your joke or story is clean and void of curse words.

- ◆ Don't use jokes or stories that stereotype race, age, ethnicity, gender, or other characteristics of people.

- ◆ Use humor to be inclusive, not exclusive. Not all learners may get the joke if you make a humorous remark about a current event or an old movie. Keep their frames of reference in mind.

If telling stories and using humor isn't your strength, it's OK not to do it. Take advantage of your own uniqueness. Are you a juggler, an amateur magician, a poet, a songwriter, or an artist? Use your unique talents to make learning points.

 ## What to Do Next

Reflect on the principles of adult learning. Ascertain the degree you utilize those principles in your facilitation of training. Specifically, what can you do to incorporate additional adult learning principles in your facilitation? Next, consider the roles of a facilitator. To what degree do you model these five roles? Which role do you need to strengthen? How will you do this? Third, consider the listing of facilitator competencies. In what area are you strong? Where do you need to improve? How will you do this? Last, how do you personalize courseware you are asked to facilitate?

◆ ◆ ◆

In the following chapter, you'll focus on the advanced training program to develop skilled facilitators.

◆

Two-Day Program: Advanced Facilitation Skills Training

What's in This Chapter?

- ◆ Objectives for facilitating a two-day workshop for learning facilitators

- ◆ Detailed program agenda

- ◆ Comprehensive teaching notes for presenting a two-day training session on facilitation skills

This chapter contains a comprehensive, step-by-step guide for conducting a learning experience for learning facilitators. It is, in essence, a "a course within a course" or, to use the more traditional term, a "train-the-trainer" course. Although time is spent on creating the climate for learning and on understanding the audience, most of this workshop is focused on helping your learners develop and practice learning facilitation skills. Your participants will learn specific techniques to conduct and debrief learning activities, ways to manage disruptive participants, methods to manage assessments, and ways to use various forms of media to enhance learning. This workshop also provides the opportunity for skill practice with feedback.

This chapter gives you, the workshop facilitator, a listing of all the materials and support requirements, learning activities, and handouts for a successful delivery.

Two-Day Program

LEARNING OBJECTIVES

- ◆ Assess one's knowledge and confidence levels regarding facilitator competencies, and identify those competencies most in need of development.

- Identify participant learning styles and preferences, and implement facilitation techniques to accommodate them.

- Analyze various types of learning activities.

- Facilitate a structured bridge activity.

- Facilitate a guided discussion.

- Develop strategies to facilitate learning while handling the needs of disruptive participants.

- Develop strategies to adjust on the fly when needed in a learning event.

- Prepare development plan strategies for practicing facilitation skills back on the job.

MATERIALS

For the facilitator/instructor:

- PowerPoint slide presentation, *Two-Day.ppt* (slides 3–1 through 3–28). To access slides for this program, open Two-Day.ppt on the accompanying CD; thumbnail copies of the slides for this workshop are included at the end of this chapter.

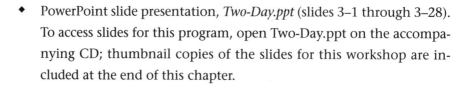

- Learning Activity 5–1: Presenters and Facilitators

- Learning Activity 5–2: Facilitator Self-Assessment

- Learning Activity 5–3: Applying Learning Styles to Facilitation of Learning Experiences

- Learning Activity 5–4: Structured Bridge Activities

- Learning Activity 5–5: Skill Practices Case Study

- Learning Activity 5–6: Facilitating Learning Activities Practice Setup

- Learning Activity 5–7: Facilitating Learning Activities Practice

- Learning Activity 5–8: Room Setup

- Learning Activity 5–9: Managing Disruptive Participants

- Learning Activity 5–10: Adjusting on the Fly

- Learning Activity 5–11: Structuring the Development Plan

◆ projector, screen, and computer for displaying PowerPoint slides, or, alternatively, overhead transparencies and overhead projector

◆ wallboard or prepared flipchart—"Parking Lot" (post on a wall prior to beginning the workshop)

◆ facilitator bio

◆ flipcharts (two for the facilitator and an appropriate number for participants to share in group activities)

◆ water-based color markers and dry-erase markers for facilitator and participants

◆ masking tape

◆ sticky-notes

◆ tent cards

◆ colored paper

◆ blank transparencies

◆ scissors.

For the participants:

◆ Handout 6–1: Presenter and Facilitator: What's the Difference?

◆ Handout 6–2: Facilitator Self-Assessment

◆ Handout 6–3: Factors for Room Setup

◆ Handout 6–4: Aligning Learning Activities and Media with Learning Preferences

◆ Handout 6–5: Learning Styles

◆ Handout 6–6: Recognizing Learning Styles

◆ Handout 6–7: Aligning Learning Activities with Learning Preferences and Styles

◆ Handout 6–8: The Interactive Lecture

◆ Handout 6–9: The Guided Discussion

◆ Handout 6–10: The Structured Bridge Activity

◆ Handout 6–11: Facilitation Case Study

- Handout 6–12: The Case Study

- Handout 6–13: The Role Play

- Handout 6–14: The Demonstration and Practice

- Handout 6–15: Behavioral Checklist for a Structured Bridge Activity

- Handout 6–16: Behavioral Checklist for a Guided Discussion

- Handout 6–17: Setting Up Instructions and Monitoring Learning Activities (Partial)

- Handout 6–18: Grouping Learners in Learning Activities (Partial)

- Handout 6–19: Sequencing Learning Activities and Giving Feedback (Partial)

- Handout 6–20: Using Media (Partial)

- Handout 6–21: Physical Presentation Tips (Partial)

- Handout 6–22: Setting Up Instructions and Monitoring Learning Activities (Complete)

- Handout 6–23: Grouping Learners in Learning Activities (Complete)

- Handout 6–24: Sequencing Learning Activities and Giving Feedback (Complete)

- Handout 6–25: Using Media (Complete)

- Handout 6–26: Physical Presentation Tips (Complete)

- Handout 6–27: Checklist for Room Setup

- Handout 6–28: Sample Room Layouts

- Handout 6–29: Room Setup Considerations

- Handout 6–30: Tips for Room Setup

- Handout 6–31: Strategies for Dealing with Disruptive Behavior

- Handout 6–32: Recognizing and Responding to Disruptive Learner Behavior

- Handout 6–33: Recommended Strategies to Deal with Disruptive Behaviors

- Handout 6–34: A Comprehensive Response for Dealing with Disruptive Behaviors

- Handout 6–35: Factors in Adjusting on the Fly

- Handout 6–36: Sample Module Plan—Creating the Climate and Environment for Learning

- Handout 6–37: Advanced Facilitation Skills Training Course Evaluation

- Handout 6–38: Facilitation Skills Training Course Evaluation

- Handout 6–39: Sample Module Plan—Skill Practices Case Study

- Handout 6–40: Structuring the Development Plan.

USING THE CD

Materials for this training session are provided in this workbook and as electronic files on the accompanying CD. To access the electronic files, insert the CD and click on the appropriate Adobe.pdf or PowerPoint.ppt/.pps document. Further directions and help in locating and using the files can be found in Appendix C: Using the Compact Disc.

AGENDA: DAY 1

8:00 a.m.   Welcome and Introductions (5 minutes)

Have slide 3–1 showing as learners enter the room. Welcome each participant individually.

Introduce yourself *briefly*. Refer to your bio, already in their materials or lying at their tables as a source of additional information about you.

Explain that this course is somewhat different from other courses that one might take because it is a "course within a course." All of the methods used to help the learners master facilitation skills are also models of how the methods can be used by the learners themselves in facilitating their own learning events. Having said that, then, the first technique that will be modeled is beginning a course with an experiential activity so that learners are immediately engaged.

8:05   Presenters and Facilitators (20 minutes)

Conduct Learning Activity 5–1, which helps the learners immediately recognize the differences between presenting information and facilitating the actual learning of that information.

In some cases the learners will already know each other, so introductions will not be necessary (pass by that bullet on slide 3–2). When learners don't know each other, this activity is suggested as a way to start that process by allowing learners to introduce themselves in their groups. You can assure them that, as the course continues and they move into different groups, they'll eventually meet everyone. Alternatively, you can have participants introduce themselves one by one as they share a thought on a difference between a presenter and a learning facilitator. This is a viable alternative activity only with a group of less than 10 people. It's not recommended for larger groups for two reasons: (a) it quickly becomes nonparticipatory and boring as each person takes a turn and everyone else must remain silent, and (b) in larger groups, some learners will be uncomfortable speaking up in front of others at this early stage in the course.

Note: *Learners tend to pay more attention to the time limit in an activity if the time is an unusual number, rather than a multiple of 5—such as 10 minutes, 15 minutes, and so on.*

Debrief Learning Activity 5–1, using slide 3–3.

One hallmark of true facilitation is that, as much as possible, the facilitator doesn't separate himself or herself from the learner audience—he or she is with the learners in the experience all the way. The facilitator is one of them, yet not one of them, and guides them to the learning destination. It's a different role from a teacher/instructor/presenter in a classroom, where there is a clear and obvious separation between the learners and the presenter, and in which the presenter is positioned as an expert who knows all while the learners are passive recipients of the knowledge. The facilitator knows the subject area, absolutely! But more than that, the facilitator is concerned with helping the learners know and apply the subject matter. The facilitator's goal is not simply to inform, but also to equip the learners for self-development and growth, for continual learning about the subject to the point of mastery.

There are five main characteristics that differentiate facilitators from presenters:

1. *The facilitator keeps the focus on the learner.* When you observe both a presentation and a facilitated learning event, many obvious differences appear. One of the most important differences, however, is one that is not visible: the *focus*. In a presentation, the focus is on the presenter. All of the materials, the presenter's behaviors, and the actions are centered on the presenter. The goals for the presentation are to cover the material, and to showcase the presenter's expertise and skill. Conversely, in a facilitated learning event the focus is on the learner. All of the materials, the facilitator's behaviors, and the activities are centered on helping learners learn and apply the content. The goal here is simple and profound: make the learning and application happen.

2. *Facilitators share control.* A presenter presents information or content to the audience. A good presenter has excellent command of language and vocabulary, an engaging speaking style, and a command of the subject. By definition, an excellent presentation results in the audience being informed about the subject matter and taking away useful information. Because the presentation centers on the presenter, that person is in control of the subject and how the audience engages with the subject (or not). The presenter decides when questions are allowed, and which questions to address. Most of the action is on the part of the presenter; the audience remains largely passive. By exercising this control, the presenter takes on full responsibility for the audience's increase in knowledge—or not. The presenter has no guarantee that the listeners will use the information or learn from it.

Effective learning facilitation, however, only *begins* with content expertise and presentation skills. An effective facilitator gives up much of the control of the content to the learner audience, and shares responsibility for the learning with them. The facilitator establishes the climate, learning structure, and flow of the learning. The learners have a great deal of flexibility in asking and responding to questions, engaging the facilitator and peer learners in discussion, and applying the content to their jobs.

3. *Facilitators derive credibility from more than subject matter expertise.* A presenter gains (or loses) her or his credibility in the minds of the audience based on the content of the presentation, on her or his mastery of that content, and on relating the content to learners' relevant experience. The presenter's ability to give examples, tell "war stories," and answer questions from a strong background and experience results in "expert" credibility. When a presenter doesn't know the answer to a question, or when the presenter's answer and the learner's experiences aren't in sync, credibility in the eyes of the audience is damaged or disappears altogether.

Whereas content expertise and control provide credibility for presenters, what facilitators *do* with these components is what creates credibility for them. Facilitator credibility is derived from

   ◆ creating and sustaining a supportive learning environment

   ◆ linking the learning to the learners' jobs

   ◆ keeping the spotlight on the learners

   ◆ being flexible and adjusting the content to the learners' needs in the moment

   ◆ helping learners "self-discover" the content.

When the facilitator is (rarely, of course!) asked a question that he or she can't answer, the facilitator helps the group find the answer together and, by doing so, retains and even increases credibility. Alternatively, if the facilitator doesn't know the answer, but has the confidence to say, "I don't know, but I'll find out," it will not damage credibility.

4. *Accountability for learning is shared.* The learners have a great deal of flexibility in asking and responding to questions, engaging the facilitator and their peer learners in discussion, and applying the content to their jobs. Because control is jointly held, accountability for learning also is joint. Not being passive, the learners are accountable both to learn and to apply the content as the facilitator guides the learning and application.

5. *Learning happens at multiple levels.* As the learners gain more control, the facilitator builds on the learners' experiences, engaging with and applying the content. Whereas presentation occurs at the thinking level, facilitation occurs at multiple levels: thinking, feeling, intuitive, physical, synergistic, and emotional. The facilitator must respond to, keep track of, and invite learner involvement at all of these levels as the learning event proceeds. And the paradox is this: the more control that's given to the learners, the more real learning occurs.

When groups share their work, "round-robin" style is strongly suggested. In this method, one group shares one item that they discussed, then the next group shares one item, then the next group, and so on. Learners can be instructed to share another of their items if a previous group shared one it already had, or they can add special emphasis to an item (and the facilitator places an extra checkmark next to the item on the chart). If there are multiple items to share (for example, if the groups were asked to answer three questions), share answers to each question by starting with a different group each time so different groups get to be first. Doing so produces the following results:

◆ *All learners remain participants throughout the sharing of information because each group doesn't have to wait long to share.*

◆ *All learners feel that their information is given equal importance.*

◆ *All learners feel that they had important information to share; when one group shares all its information before moving on to the next group, the last groups to share often have no new contributions to make. They feel their participation wasn't important and the other groups "stole their thunder."*

8:25   Complete Course Introduction (5 minutes)

Share information about the course schedule, facilities, and any other "housekeeping" issues.

Show slides 3–4 and 3–5. Ask for a show of hands regarding which objectives are the most desired by the group. This will give you a sense of what material can be handled more quickly and which sections will need more time. Your emphasis will differ each time you facilitate this workshop because it's always based on the learners' stated needs.

8:30   Norms/Standard Operating Procedures/Ground Rules (20 minutes)

Explain that there is a lot of content and application to be experienced over the next two days. To accomplish this, you'll want to establish some ground rules.

Ask the participants, "What are some group norms, standard operating procedures, or ground rules that will help us work together to make this a great learning experience?" Record responses on a flipchart page and post it on a wall. Explain that when they facilitate learning, ground rules can be pointed out to help manage the agenda and participant behavior.

As you record their responses, be sure these ground rules are included:

♦ Start/stop on time, including breaks and lunches

♦ Don't hold private conversations

♦ Stay on topic

♦ Participate and share insights

♦ Respect others' opinions and time to talk

- ◆ "Pass" if you wish when asked to respond

- ◆ More experienced participants may coach others

- ◆ Maintain confidentiality—what happens in here stays in here

- ◆ Turn off cell phones and pagers

- ◆ Have fun.

How do you "make sure" certain points are included? When the group falls silent, say, "I have a suggestion—what do you think?" and insert one of your desired items. If a participant volunteers an item that's similar to one you want to see posted, ask, "Do you mean . . . ?" and write it that way, with the participant's permission.

Refer to your pre-posted wallchart titled "Parking Lot." It can be a sketch or a graphic image of a parking lot with three rows of spaces, labeled "Short-term," "Long-term," and "Valet." Explain that the parking lot is the place for participants to "park" questions until a more appropriate time to answer them. Indicate that the participants are to use the sticky-notes to write their questions and place them in the appropriate column on the chart: short-term = I need an answer today, long-term = I need an answer sometime during the training program, and valet = I need an answer in the near future after the course is finished.

We suggest that you gather and address the sticky-notes after breaks or at the end of the day. Address each note by answering the question, or by explaining when and how you will answer the question.

8:50 Break (10 minutes)

9:00 Facilitator Competencies (30 minutes)

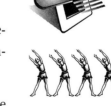

Show slide 3–6. Introduce facilitator competencies by reviewing the competency categories on the slide. Conduct Learning Activity 5–2.

When the partner discussions are complete, draw the group back together. Take a poll of the participants to identify which items are problematic for the greatest number of them. This will give you additional informa-

tion about what material can be handled quickly, and which sections will need more time. Your emphasis each time you facilitate this workshop will be different because it's based on the learners' stated needs.

After completing the poll, explain that one of the key expectations of an effective facilitator is the creation of an environment that's conducive to learning for all learners.

9:30   Creating the Climate for Learning (30 minutes)

Explain that the climate for learning doesn't just happen. There are several aspects to creating such a climate:

- ◆ setting up the room and adjusting the physical environment before the learning event

- ◆ preparing yourself for the facilitation experience

- ◆ greeting the learners as they arrive

- ◆ making the learners feel comfortable as they arrive

- ◆ conducting opening activities.

Conduct the following guided discussion about physical environment.

Guided discussion question: How a room is set up is an important part of creating the learning climate and can be an important factor in enhancing—or hindering—the learning. Some examples will help clarify these limits. Example 1: You're delivering a workshop in a hotel. The hotel indicates that the room will hold up to 30. Because you only expect 20 participants, there should be plenty of room, right? Is there a potential problem?

- ◆ *Likely learner response:* The hotel might mean it holds 30 in rows of chairs, for example, but not for a learning-type arrangement.

- ◆ *Augmenting comments:* Many hotels determine the room capacity by lecture style. You can get many more people in a room set lecture style than you can in rounds or a U-shaped setup. In addition, the capacity does not tell you the room's dimensions. Many hotel rooms are rectangular and narrow with columns, which presents problems with participants' line of sight.

Guided discussion question: Example 2: You're taking a workshop to another company location. They have a training room that's the right size and has the media requirements. They tell you that they use the room for training. Through some later discussion, you realize that it's computer skills training that the room is used for. What's the issue?

◆ *Likely learner response:* Computer stations could get in the way of participants' using their materials.

◆ *Augmenting comments:* Also, fixed desks support lecture style of delivery. This limits your capability to do small group work and lead facilitative discussion.

Guided discussion question: Example 3: What are the considerations if you want to use small breakout rooms for separate small group work?

◆ *Likely learner response:* Make sure there are enough rooms for each group.

◆ *Augmenting comments:* Breakout rooms provide a good environment for group activities. Make sure that the rooms have the necessary supplies. For example, if you want the learners to produce flipcharts for later presentation in another room, and the participants used the whiteboards in the room instead, you have a problem. In addition, if the breakout rooms are on different floors, it's more difficult to monitor and coach the various groups.

Guided discussion question: Example 4: Some locations have an executive boardroom that you can use. Many times, these rooms are auditorium-and-pit style (auditorium style with raised rows as you move from the front to the back). What's the issue?

◆ *Likely learner response:* Everyone is facing forward so they won't be able to interact with each other.

◆ *Augmenting comments:* Such rooms are good for making presentations, but not good for facilitating learning. It would be difficult to have small group work or even triads. Additionally, the room may be too large for the group, losing intimacy.

These scenarios tell us that we must do our research and be sure the room is appropriate for the type of learning experience. Therefore, find out the true usability of a room before delivery.

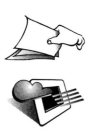

Distribute Handout 6–3 and reveal slide 3–7. Complete the guided discussion by discussing the handout and slide.

The following is a list of things to consider when selecting or reserving a training room:

◆ The number of participants gives you initial insight into the size of room and type of learning activities.

◆ Types of learning activities demand certain accommodations.

◆ The number of teams prompts consideration regarding room size and breakout sessions.

◆ Physical limitations of the room will influence activities and media use.

◆ Room arrangement will affect how you organize your materials, where and how you stand, and so on—all the aspects of your personal space.

◆ The more bodies in the room, the higher the temperature will rise.

◆ Anything you add to the environment in an effort to enhance learning constitutes peripheral materials and methods.

◆ Where you place refreshments should allow easy access and a natural flow in getting and fixing the food and drinks.

◆ Learner setup, groupings, and table shapes will have a significant effect on the learning environment. (We'll visit this in detail later on.)

10:00 Learning Preferences and Learning Styles (55 minutes, including a 10-minute break when convenient)

Conduct an interactive lecture on learning preferences, supported by slide 3–8. The text on the slide provides the content you'll review in your interactive lecture.

Learning preference relates to how people take in information. There are three main categories: visual, auditory, and kinesthetic. Although a good design will accommodate varied preferences, the facilitator can improve learning by tailoring facilitation methods to the learning preferences of participants:

◆ **Visual learners** take in and process information through what they see. Their preference is for printed information, pictures, graphics, and such.

◆ **Auditory learners** take in and process information that is heard, including words, alliteration, and music/songs.

◆ **Kinesthetic learners** take in and process information through physical, hands-on experiences.

On a whiteboard or on three flipcharts, write the headings: "Visual," "Auditory," and "Kinesthetic." Ask the participants for various methods to accommodate the three learning preferences. Have them identify the learning preference and provide a rationale for their alignment of method to preference. You record participants' ideas under the appropriate heading. Be sure that the ideas listed below are presented and discussed.

To meet the visual learner's preferences, your facilitation can include

- PowerPoint slides or overhead transparencies
- flipcharts
- wallboards
- demonstrations
- diagrams, charts, and drawings
- participant manuals
- reference materials
- reading assignments
- workbooks
- interactive computer simulations.

To aid the learner with an auditory preference, you can incorporate

- presentations and interactive lectures
- guided discussions
- demonstrations or group activities with feedback
- verbal instructions
- audiovisuals and video tapes
- acronyms and mnemonic devices
- songs
- background instrumental music
- panel discussions
- question-and-answer sessions
- rhymes, chants, and poetry.

To accommodate a kinesthetic learning preference, you could include

- hands-on practice
- role play

- behavior modeling

- structured note taking (learners fill in blanks on handouts)

- simulations

- individual and group activities and projects

- learner-developed materials, such as drawings, flipcharts, and posters

- interactive computer simulations.

Distribute Handout 6–4. Explain that it provides a way for facilitators to select activities according to how participants take in information—that is, their learning preferences.

Refer participants to Appendix B: Using Media. That appendix suggests when to use certain media, offers tips for their use, and points out some advantages and disadvantages of various media types.

Pass out Handout 6–5. Conduct an interactive lecture on learning styles, supported by slides 3–9 through 3–14.

In addition to learning preferences, your participants also have preferred learning styles.

Learning styles relate to how learners process information. There are five learner styles: achievers, evaluators, networkers, observers, and socializers.

- **Achievers** focus on doing and accomplishing results and are good at finding practical uses for ideas and theories. They enjoy being involved in new and challenging experiences and carrying out plans to meet those challenges. Achievers have the ability to solve problems, make decisions, and develop action plans based on implementing solutions to questions or problems. Achievers like to accept the lead role in addressing those challenges.

They like sequence and logical order and clear, step-by-step directions. Achievers are not strongly people oriented and have a tendency to take control with little regard for others' feelings.

◆ **Evaluators** like to analyze a situation and use a logical process to resolve issues. They ask many detailed questions and, in doing so, collect a great deal of information. They're very concerned about working within the existing guidelines. Evaluators are good at assimilating a wide range of information and putting it into concise, logical forms, such as lists, charts, or planning tools. These learners are more interested in the basis of theory and application of theory, and less interested in building relationships. The theory you present to them must be logically sound, exact, and supported by facts.

◆ **Networkers** like to develop close relationships with others and avoid interpersonal conflict. Their good listening skills enable them to develop strong people networks. Networkers are more compliant than others; they are easily swayed, try to avoid risks, seek consensus, and are slower than others in making decisions. In group activities, networkers seldom disagree with others' opinions; rather, they're supportive of others and seek collaboration. They take time to build trust and get personally acquainted with others. While outgoing, they need direct feedback as a way of support.

◆ **Socializers** like to talk and share. They like the spotlight and want to have fun. Although they welcome multiple perspectives, they're good at selling their ideas to others and building alliances. Socializers aren't concerned with details or facts; they like to keep a fast pace and make quick, spontaneous decisions. In group work, the socializer wants to work quickly, seek others' input, persuade others, get the task done quickly, provide some humor, and volunteer to make the presentation.

◆ **Observers** are best at viewing concrete situations from many different points of view. They prefer to watch and conceptualize rather than take action. They're reflective thinkers. They enjoy situations that call for generating not just many ideas, but also a wide range of ideas. These learners are more interested in abstract ideas and concepts, and less interested in building relationships. Observers don't like to wing it.

Conduct Learning Activity 5–3. Distribute Handout 6–6 as an aid for their group work. (Activity directions are on slide 3–15.)

After the learner groups have presented their answers, distribute Handout 6–7.

Debrief Learning Activity 5–3. As the groups present, affirm and augment their answers by ensuring that all the techniques listed below are covered.

For Achievers:

◆ Provide step-by-step directions and specific outcomes for all learning activities.

◆ Debrief case studies, role play, and action learning by emphasizing the real-world situations.

◆ Allow adequate time for the development of action plans for on-the-job application of the new knowledge, skills, and abilities.

◆ In facilitative discussions and presentations, emphasize the link to the job in real-world terms—what works on the job.

◆ Begin the learning experience with a review of a performance contract, providing application of the course content. Revisit the performance contract often.

◆ Because achievers are take-charge people, rotate small group leadership roles to give other learners a chance.

◆ If needed, revisit course ground rules concerning everyone's participation, mutual respect, and the value of others' opinions.

For Evaluators:

◆ Provide a summary of the theoretical basis of the content.

◆ When debriefing activities, build on the results and then provide application to the job.

◆ Facilitate case studies, individual projects, and reading or research, providing a theoretical base for your response; provide visuals, such as charts or diagrams.

◆ Apply theory to learning activities and to the job.

◆ In a group activity, provide detailed instructions, outcomes, and the format for presentations.

◆ Provide sources of information and access to that information to support learning activities.

◆ Present the value and job-relatedness of learning activities and course content.

For Networkers:

◆ Allow them to take the lead in ice-breaking activities.

◆ Stimulate group interaction and involvement by asking what they think of others' ideas.

◆ Provide direct feedback to their comments and contributions to group projects.

◆ Provide them with opportunities for interaction in small groups and one-on-one activities.

◆ Use peer teaching and tutoring.

For Socializers:

- Use their outgoing nature to stimulate group interaction.

- Keep the learning content and learning activities moving.

- Indicate that not all learners are as fast as they are when it comes to learning new ideas and skills.

- When providing instructions, remind them that the process of arriving at decisions is as important as the decisions themselves.

- Remind them that a presentation requires depth; superficial responses are not enough.

- Ask socializers for their rationale or for the facts behind their comments. Strive to take them deeper into the content.

- In large group discussions, recognize their contributions but ask for alternative views.

- Use socializers in brainstorming activities.

For Observers:

- Incorporate demonstrations, case studies, and brainstorming into the learning activities.

- Provide an opportunity for individual work first, before group work.

- Incorporate "what-if" scenarios and open-ended questions, and write the responses on a flipchart.

- Have them present their process for solving a case and the lessons learned; link their ideas back to the course content.

- Allow for reflection following learning activities.

- Provide time for participants to reflect on what they have experienced, and to make some notes about the meaning of those experiences and their application to the job or situation.

♦ Debrief activities by building on the results and going into more abstract ideas, such as generating future situations.

Now that we've discussed and applied several concepts regarding the room setup and your participants, we want to move into in-depth material and skill building on facilitating learning activities. As we discuss and practice these facilitation methods and techniques, make a mental note of how they align with the different learning preferences and styles.

10:55   The Interactive Lecture Learning Activity (25 minutes)

Explain to your participants that the remainder of Day 1 will be spent in learning about various types of learning activities, and about the components of learning that support them. Tell them that you'll begin with the **interactive lecture** learning activity.

The next four activities will be recursive—that is, the participants will learn about an activity by actually participating in it. This means that you'll be conducting an interactive lecture about the interactive lecture learning activity, you'll facilitate a guided discussion about the guided discussion learning activity, you'll facilitate a structured bridge activity about the structured bridge learning activity, and you'll facilitate a case study about case studies and other complex learning activities.

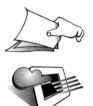

Distribute Handout 6–8 and display slide 3–16. For the next 10 minutes, conduct an interactive lecture about the interactive lecture activity. As you present information about this method, pause and ask the learners questions—and invite their questions—periodically throughout the activity. You may use the following questions at intervals as you deliver the content:

♦ Who has experienced a lecture in the past?

♦ What are the pros and cons of a lecture as a learning activity?

♦ Why would we want learner participation during a lecture?

- ◆ How would you add the "interactive" element to this activity?

- ◆ In what types of situations should the interactive lecture be used?

The foundation of all skills is knowledge, and learners must know before they do. A traditional lecture applies to learners who don't have any (or have very little) background in the content of the lesson or course. It's an activity characterized by the participants' relative passivity (they're usually listening, reading, or observing without interacting); by more focus on the facilitator (who must deliver the content because the audience members don't know it); and (usually) by individual rather than group work.

It's important to make a lecture interactive—hence the name. Even learners who know very little about the content can respond to questions that engage them at a level they can understand and that relate to their own experiences.

To make a lecture interactive, the facilitator presents content (a mini-lecture lasting a few minutes), and then invites participation by asking the learners questions and by inviting their questions. The facilitator continues to share content and invite participation throughout the entire activity. By inviting listeners to take part, what is normally thought of as a lecture *by* the facilitator becomes an interactive lecture *with* the learners. Interactive lecture should be used when learners know relatively little about the content, and therefore must learn about it before they can interact with it.

Here are some tips for using this activity:

- ◆ Plan the intervals at which you might ask the participants if they have questions.

- ◆ Plan a couple of your key questions intended to gain participation.

◆ Never deliver a "straight lecture" for more than 10–15 minutes without inviting participation in some way.

Interactive lecture is part of a category of learning activities that focus on disseminating content, and in which learners are relatively passive. Other such activities include

- ◆ reading books, handouts

- ◆ watching videos/films; viewing PowerPoint presentations, slides, overhead transparencies

- ◆ completing pre-work

- ◆ taking notes

- ◆ completing self-assessments, such as checklists and quizzes.

The same principles for creating interaction and engagement can be used during facilitation of those activities.

11:20   The Guided Discussion Learning Activity (30 minutes)

Now you will conduct a **guided discussion** *about* guided discussions. Below are several questions for you to raise with your learners as you facilitate the discussion. These questions are accompanied by likely responses and some additional comments pertinent to each question.

Remember that a guided discussion is a planned discussion in which the facilitator prepares questions that will guide learners into "discovery" of the learning points. The facilitator asks specific, planned questions to draw learning points from the learners. You augment their responses by making more in-depth learning points.

Guided discussion question: What comes to your mind when you hear the term *guided discussion*?

- ◆ *Likely learner response:* Facilitator is guiding participants in a certain direction.

- ◆ *Augmenting comment:* Yes, that's right, and it's done with open-ended questions.

Guided discussion question: What do you think is the difference between an interactive lecture and a guided discussion?

- *Likely learner response:* In an interactive lecture, most of the content still comes from the facilitator. In a guided discussion, it's more even.

- *Augmenting comment:* Correct. There is more learner engagement in a guided discussion. And questions are preplanned and matched to specific learning points, rather than simply interjected on the fly as they are in the interactive lecture.

Guided discussion question: Why do you think learners can be more engaged in a guided discussion than in the previous type of activity?

- *Likely learner response:* They know more about the content, so they can participate more.

- *Augmenting comment:* So, the facilitator has to do a good job ahead of time in determining how much the learners know so the guided discussion can be chosen in the right situation.

Guided discussion question: How does a facilitator "do" a guided discussion?

- *Likely learner response:* Plans questions ahead of time.

- *Augmenting comment:* Not only the questions—the facilitator also plans on what the learners' most likely responses are, and on what augmenting content the facilitator will add.

Guided discussion question: Can you think of any time, other than when disseminating content, that a facilitator might use a guided discussion?

- *Likely learner response:* ???? (probably won't have an answer)

- *Augmenting comment:* A special type of guided discussion is called a **debrief,** and it's used after a learning activity to help the learners process what happened and what they learned. It's designed to close the gaps in the learning, to summarize the main points, and to help the learners apply the content to the job. Here are a couple typical sets of debriefing questions: What happened in the activity? How did that make you feel? What principles or generalizations can you infer from it? How will you apply it going forward? What went well? What could have been done better? How does this apply to your job? What will you do differently in the future?

Show slide 3–17 and distribute Handout 6–9. Ask learners to take a moment to read these. Ask if there were any points that had not been captured during the guided discussion you have just conducted. If any, reinforce these.

Now that we've looked at two ways to disseminate content with increased interaction, after lunch we'll take a look at the more interactive learner-centered activities.

11:50 Lunch (70 minutes)

1:00 p.m. The Structured Bridge Learning Activity (45 minutes)

Show slide 3–18. Take approximately 10 minutes to explain that the learners in structured activities work together to understand and use content at a deeper level than simple comprehension—at levels such as synthesis, integration, evaluation, and application. A **structured activity** is literally an activity in which the learners participate, usually working together. It's structured, although not led, by the facilitator. Structured activities are the "bridge of discovery" between knowledge and skills. Structured activities help learners engage with content at a deeper level by thinking through a concept, inferring from it to generate principles, and applying it to different situations or to "discover" the content that they already know.

Learners are more active and involved in a structured activity than in interactive lectures or guided discussions. The focus is on the learners, and the facilitator's role is that of organizer, monitor, and guide. These activities are used with learners who have some knowledge of the desired content and who are ready for more depth and concept application.

Facilitate Learning Activity 5–4.

After the learner groups have presented their answers, distribute Handout 6–10 and conduct a debriefing.

Here are suggested questions for a debrief discussion (as is necessary in the guided discussion format, *you* develop the likely learner responses and the augmenting comments to accompany them):

◆ What items about structured bridge activities in the handout were not in the presentations?

◆ How would you define the varied learning activities mentioned in the "Tips" section?

◆ What questions do you have?

If they have not already been made by the learners, here are points to make in the discussion:

◆ Sometimes content to support the activity has been acquired earlier in the same course. In other instances, the learners already have the content and experience when they walk into the workshop. In the latter case, the first type of activity used is often a structured activity. The learner groups are given questions to answer or a problem to solve and, in the process of doing so, they discover the new content.

◆ Often the activity is conducted before the content is revealed so the learners have the "first crack" at discovering the content within their own knowledge base. The content is then presented in a debriefing guided discussion to ensure all the points have been made.

Explain other types of structured bridge activities, such as

- ◆ **Solo work:** learners are given an assignment to work on alone (such as to fill out a questionnaire or analyze a problem); then they discuss it with others.

- ◆ **Small group discussion:** small groups of learners are given a topic to discuss or questions to answer; they work together, and then present their results.

- ◆ **Group inquiry:** the learners are provided with content, and they work together to identify questions they have about that content.

- ◆ **Information search:** learners are given reference materials and must search through them for answers to questions presented by the facilitator. In a blended learning experience (in which face-to-face learning and e-learning are combined), the process may involve using the Internet to conduct searches or to download information.

- ◆ **Small group assignment/problem solving:** small groups of learners are given a problem to solve, a situation to analyze, a list of principles or guidelines to develop in response to a problem, and so forth.

- ◆ **Peer teaching:** small groups of learners study the material, then teach it to the other participants or groups in the class. Determining the teaching methodology is part of the activity, and it's left up to the groups.

- ◆ **Games ("Jeopardy," "Bingo," "Concentration"):** a version of a popular game can be developed to assist learners in comprehending, remembering, and applying content that has been presented.

The "how to" section for structured bridge activities mentions forming learner groups and monitoring the work of learner groups. If the participants ask questions about how to do that, tell them that it will be covered in a later activity.

1:45   Advanced Structured Activities (Skill Practices) (70 minutes, including a 10-minute break when convenient)

Explain that once the learners have mastered knowledge and applied it at a deeper level in a bridge activity, the next part of the learning is skill practice. This is exactly what it says—the actual practice of the skill. If the skill is driving a car, then the skill practice is actually driving a car (or a simulator). If the skill is conducting a job interview or making a sales presentation, then the skill practice is conducting a mock interview or sales presentation. If the skill is analyzing a situation and making recommendations, then the skill practice is analyzing a case situation and making recommendations. In other words, **skill practice** is the performance of the skill, adjusted when necessary for the learning environment.

You're now going to learn about skill practices by participating in one.

Conduct Learning Activity 5–5. Distribute Handouts 6–11 through 6–14, and review the activity instructions on slide 3–20.

When 30 minutes' preparation time is up and the groups are ready to present, conduct the presentations and debriefings in the following manner. For each type of learning activity (case, role play, and demonstration and practice):

1. Have the small group make its presentation.

2. Conduct a debriefing guided discussion to share learning points that may have been missed in the presentation and to emphasize critical points (see below for each activity's learning points).

3. Review the handout that accompanies the activity (6–12 for case studies, 6–13 for role play, and 6–14 for demonstration and practice).

4. Answer any questions that remain.

Here are learning points for the case study on driving etiquette:

1. How would John set this up? What skill is addressed? What materials would he use? [This is a mental skill—deciding what to do in an etiquette-related situation. Case study, presenting problem situations, is the appropriate activity. It needs to be set up so that the learners must make etiquette decisions in situations. John would set this up as learners working together—partners, small groups, and so on. For materials, John would write etiquette for situations in which the learners must decide what to do.]

2. What would he have the learners do as part of the case study activity? [He could form small groups, assign each one a situation, and ask them to identify what they should do in each scenario. He has two needs to fill in this activity: have the learners actually practice the skill—that is, make etiquette decisions—and have them work together to share ideas.]

3. What potential pitfalls should he watch out for as he facilitates the activity? [The situations need to be realistic and not too simple. He could even develop specific questions for each scenario that the learners would answer to make it more challenging and to provoke them to analyze the skill at an even deeper level. The group sizes should be in tune with the learners' comfort levels—that is, smaller groups if the learners are still new to each other, larger groups if they are more comfortable.]

4. How will he measure the learners' success in solving the case? [The course content on etiquette would include criteria for what a good etiquette decision "looks like." For example, a good etiquette decision (a) takes all parties' needs into account, (b) is based on "rules of the road" that are commonly known, and (c) realizes when to "give" even if one is right, and so on. The criteria would

be used to examine each small group's answers to the scenarios.]

Here are the learning points for the role play on resolving a fender-bender:

1. How would John set this up? What skill is addressed? What materials would he use? [This is an interpersonal skill—interacting with another person. Role play is the appropriate activity. For materials, John would write up the scenarios according to his decision about type of role play (see below); that is, he could develop a script for the learners to read in the role play; or give them the outline of a scenario, and let them run with it.]

2. What types of role play should he consider? [John would have to make a decision as to what kind of role play should be facilitated, on a continuum from less challenging to more challenging. Factors that might influence his decision include how difficult the learners have found the content to this point— that is, the harder the content is for them, the simpler the role play; the group's comfort level with role play activities—that is, the less comfort, the simpler the role play; and whether this particular skill is process oriented with certain steps that must be followed to have a successful conversation (would lead to a more scripted role play), or is product oriented with many ways the conversation can be implemented as long as a specific result is achieved (would lead to a more improvised role play).]

3. What factors will be important for him to consider? [Learners' comfort level with role play activities; time available; number of learners; whether learners will receive feedback from the facilitator or from each other; and complexity of the content.]

4. How will he measure the learners' success in enacting the role play? [John has two choices in meas-

urement, and it depends on how the content is taught in the course: (a) if the course content implies that this skill is process oriented, then the measure would be a checklist of behavioral steps that can be checked off by an observer; (b) if the course content implies that this skill is product oriented, then the measure would be a checklist of criteria for a "good" conflict resolution conversation that could be checked off by an observer.]

Here is a list of learning points for the demonstration and practice on driving in foggy conditions:

1. How would John set this up? What skill is addressed? What materials/tools would he use? [John would have two choices here, depending on the experience level of the learners: (a) if they are very inexperienced in driving, he might use a simpler wheeled vehicle, such as a scooter, to demonstrate what happens to traction in foggy conditions, and the principles of handling the foggy environment, before having them practice in a real car; (b) if they are more experienced, he might use a real car in an empty parking lot to demonstrate with an opaque shield over the window to suggest foggy visibility.]

2. What would he have the learners do as part of the practice? [They would observe him as he showed them what to do. Then they would do it themselves.]

3. How will he measure the learners' success in the practice segment? [An observer using a checklist of steps to follow would observe, check off items, and give learners feedback as they practice the skill. John would have to make a decision regarding whether he, as the facilitator, must give the feedback or if the learners can give feedback to each other. With a behavioral checklist, it's relatively easy for learners to give each other feedback. Sometimes, however, it's a better fit with organization culture for the facilitator to give the feedback to each learner.]

Explain that the learners will now have the opportunity to facilitate an activity themselves, and that the setup for this skill practice is next.

2:55   Planning Learning Activities (35 minutes)

This activity, the last of the day, is designed to give the learners instructions about the skill practices they'll demonstrate in the morning, and to give them preparation time during the course.

Facilitate Learning Activity 5–6. Use slide 3–21 to form learner groups.

Learning Activity 5–6 instructs you to divide the learners into five groups. These groups should be approximately equal in size. Learners can count off to be assigned to groups randomly, or they can choose the topic on which they're most interested in working.

Use slide 3–22 to give instructions for the activity that will be facilitated in the morning. Pass out Handouts 6–15 through 6–21 as directed in the learning activity.

3:30   Preparation Time (60–90 minutes; time will vary)

After the activity has been set up, tell the learners that they will now have a "lab" during which they can design and prepare for their learning activities. Explain that you will be in the room to answer questions and make suggestions if they get stuck.

Tell them how long you'll be available and, if applicable, how long they're permitted to stay in the meeting space to do their work. Instruct them to be prepared to begin the first activity when class starts the next morning.

Have various media available for learners to use in designing their activities and materials (such as colored paper, markers, blank transparencies, scissors, and tape). Let

them know that the quality of their materials won't matter—it's the thought and designs that will.

Learners likely will be concerned about the "partial" handouts (6–17 through 6–21) and about their perceived inability to deliver two activities in 10 minutes. Here are some suggested responses:

- ◆ The partial handouts are meant to give you a head start on the information you might choose to deliver in your activities. You have a lot of knowledge and experience that will add to the handouts.

- ◆ Complete handouts will be distributed when the activity is over, so you'll have complete materials for reference.

- ◆ You'll have to limit to two or three the number of learning points that you'll cover.

- ◆ You probably want to split your time this way: approximately two-thirds on a structured bridge activity and one-third on a debriefing guided discussion.

- ◆ This is a microcosm of real-world application; we never have enough time to deliver the content that we want to deliver.

AGENDA: DAY 2

8:00 a.m.   Facilitating Learning Activities Practice (3 hours, plus two 10-minute breaks when convenient)

Facilitate Learning Activity 5–7.

This activity is recursive in two ways: (a) the learners are learning the skills for the structured bridge activity and the guided discussion by actually practicing them, and (b) they're learning about other aspects of facilitation (setting up and structuring learning activities, grouping learners in learning activities, pacing and monitoring learning activities, using media, and physical presentation) by participating in activities about that content.

This activity is planned to take three hours (180 minutes): 30 minutes each for five group facilitations, and 30 minutes for a large group debriefing discussion. The 30 minutes for each facilitation should be used in the following fashion:

- ◆ 5 minutes to set up.

- ◆ 10 minutes for the learners to facilitate the activity.

- ◆ 5 minutes to facilitate a short feedback session in a format of "what went well and what could be improved?" The presenting group can comment first, followed by other learners. As the facilitator, you add any final comments.

- ◆ 5 minutes for learners to fill in the checklists with their comments and give them to the presenting group.

- ◆ 5 minutes to distribute the "Complete" handouts (6–22 through 6–26) for the learning activity content that applies to that presentation and to have learners review the handout briefly to see if any additional points should be brought out.

Plan to take two 10-minute breaks at suitable points during this time span (for example, at 9:00 and 10:30), bringing the total time for the activity to 3 hours, 20 minutes.

When all group facilitations have been completed (at approximately 10:50 a.m.), facilitate a large group debriefing discussion. Remember that you are debriefing two experiences: the facilitation experience with guided discussion and structured bridge activity, and the content that learners discovered regarding the other topics.

Here are some suggested guided questions:

- ◆ What went well in *developing* the guided discussion and structured bridge activities?

  - ◆ What were your biggest challenges in *developing* the guided discussion and structured bridge activities? How did you overcome them?

  - ◆ What would you do differently the next time?

- What general principles can you infer about *developing* these activities?

- What went well in *facilitating* the guided discussion and structured bridge activities?

  - What were your biggest challenges in *facilitating* the guided discussion and structured bridge activities? How did you overcome them?

  - What would you do differently the next time?

  - What general principles can you infer about *facilitating* these activities?

- What was new information for you regarding setting up and structuring learning activities?

  - What will you do differently going forward?

- What was new information for you regarding grouping learners in learning activities?

  - What will you do differently going forward?

- What was new information for you regarding pacing and monitoring learning activities?

  - What will you do differently going forward?

- What was new information for you regarding using media?

  - What will you do differently going forward?

- What was new information for you regarding physical presentation?

  - What will you do differently going forward?

 *Many of the learners' answers to these questions will be specific to their experience, so as you augment their responses and continue the activity, go with the flow. In addition to the actual content on the "complete" handouts, however, common themes to expect in their answers (or for you to make sure are brought out) include the following:*

- *Facilitation is harder than it looks.*

◆ *It's a good thing to have models and methods to follow so you don't have to reinvent the wheel each time.*

◆ *Facilitation is multilayered; many aspects come together to support the learning in the moment.*

◆ *The facilitator's focus is on all the layers of what is happening at the time; an apt analogy is the director of a play.*

Refer to "Facilitation Guidelines," on the accompanying CD, for tips to enhance facilitation skills.

Tell learners that during the various activities they've probably noticed how room and seating arrangements affect learning. Explain that this will be the focus now.

11:20 Room and Seating Setup (40 minutes)

Facilitate Learning Activity 5–8, using slide 3–23 and Handouts 6–27 and 6–28.

When the participants have concluded their presentation, you want to ensure that their designs include the basics, such as

◆ a front table for facilitator's guide, media, and projector. Depending on the media support, the projector may be a computer projection system with the media on a CD, or it may be an overhead projector with transparencies of PowerPoint slides. In either case, the projector could be on a cart inside the "U" or on the facilitator's table. Refer to "Media Checklist," on the accompanying CD. Explain that it should be used as a job aid to ensure that the facilitator has considered all media implications.

◆ a door at the back of the room.

◆ no podium.

- a side table for handouts and program materials.

- a screen behind and just to the side of the facilitator's table.

- a table for refreshments, against a wall and behind the seating.

A U-style setup will enable participants to interact, the facilitator to move among the participants, individual work to be done, and pairs to work together.

Note: Even if you had an activity with a group of three people, two could remain seated and the third could move a chair inside the U to face the other two. Because the design of the course calls for (a) some individual work, (b) working in pairs, and (c) some small group work, the U shape allows for interaction and pairs, while team work can be accomplished with the team tables in the back.

The remaining issue is to allow for larger group work. Because the room is larger than needed, place team tables in the back of the room. This provides a place for the larger groups to meet and conduct their group activities, and includes the advantage of not having "dead space" in the room that hinders group cohesiveness. Given the size of the room, there should be enough wall space by the team tables for posting group work.

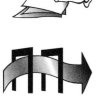

Close this section by distributing Handouts 6–29 and 6–30, indicating that these are tips to help ensure that the environment enhances learning.

Now that we've looked at many important factors that influence learning effectiveness, after lunch we'll take a look at two critical factors: managing the disruptive participant and adjusting on the fly.

Noon   Lunch (60 minutes)

1:00 p.m.   Managing Disruptive Participants (60–65 minutes)

Explain that there are several types of learners in any learning environment, including

- people who wish to learn and are there voluntarily

- those who want to hone a skill or pick up new ideas

- people sent by their managers

- those who are simply taking a break from the daily grind.

No matter which group participants belong to, they're all trying to fulfill their needs and agendas. Some of these needs and agendas are related to the learning, and some are not. When participants act to fulfill a non-learning-related need, we tend to label them "difficult" because their behavior can disrupt the learning for themselves and others. Disruptive behavior occurs when a participant acts according to his or her individual needs or agenda and, as a result, the learning of other participants is minimized.

Facilitate Learning Activity 5–9.

Here are some answers you can expect when the learners describe typical disruptive behavior (be sure to make some of these points if they don't):

- engaging in side conversation

- talking too much, monopolizing discussion

- complaining, being negative about the class or the organization

- daydreaming, not really being "in the class"

- heckling the facilitator

- challenging the facilitator on content or technique, being a "know-it-all"

- telling jokes or clowning around at inappropriate times

- making an inappropriate remark (sexist, racist, and such)

- doing other work, reading the newspaper, or making/taking cell phone calls

- remaining silent, not participating verbally

- withdrawing from the group interpersonally, physically, or both

- going off on a tangent, missing the point.

Conduct a debrief discussion using Handouts 6–31 and 6–32.

Here are some of the most likely causes for those behaviors (that is, the learner's personal agenda):

- learner is bored

- learner is not engaged in the work

- learner is distracted by external matters

- learner is unhappy about the organization and is using the class as an opportunity to vent

- learner wants attention, the spotlight

- learner wants to be acknowledged for expertise

- learner is uncomfortable with the subject matter

- learner is shy, reserved.

The underlying causal factor for most disruptive behavior is that the participant has a personal agenda she or he is supporting. Why do some people end up labeled as difficult participants? For example, say that a participant challenges your expertise in front of the class because of his personal agenda of wanting to be acknowledged for his expertise. This behavior is not directed at you, and it's not about you—but it feels like it is!

In that situation, it's very easy for you to react personally. A personal agenda arises on your part, which might be to prove your own expertise and avoid damaging (or possibly even enhance) your own credibility in front of the class. So, a behavior arises out of your own personal agenda, and you get into a debate with the participant. Who wins? No one!

Your response to difficult behavior must be depersonalized. To begin, rather than label people "difficult participants," call it "disruptive behavior." In this way, you're labeling the behavior—not the person. Then, your actions must focus always on helping the learning occur. To do that, you must strive to meet that person's agenda. Counterintuitive as that feels, it's usually true that when you meet that person's agenda, the agenda goes away, and the disruptive behavior is extinguished.

Complete Learning Activity 5–9 to develop the strategies for addressing disruptive behavior. Review its depiction of what must happen in a facilitator's thought processes when disruptive behavior occurs.

Distribute Handout 6–33 and Handout 6–34. Ask the learners to spend a few minutes of solo time reviewing the handouts. Invite questions.

Conduct a short interactive lecture, reviewing the points on slide 3–25. In general, facilitator tactics for handling disruptive behavior should include

- ◆ not getting caught in one-on-one power struggles

- ◆ using good-natured humor

- ◆ connecting with the participant on a personal level

- ◆ broadening the participation of the rest of the group

- ◆ protecting participants as needed

- ◆ using a separate "Issues Chart" or a "Parking Lot" to postpone issues until they are appropriate for discussion

- ◆ recognizing the learner's point and then taking the discussion off-line during breaks, lunches, and at the end of the day

- ◆ changing the small group composition

- ◆ modifying activities or instructional strategies.

There are many things that can get a learning event off track from a schedule standpoint; participant behavior is only one factor. Sometimes activities take longer than planned, or participants can't seem to return from lunch or breaks on time, or you got started a little later than you intended. Whatever the reason, there are times when you'll need to make adjustments to get back on schedule. The next section, Adjusting on the Fly, is designed to help you do that.

2:05   Break (10 minutes)

2:15   Adjusting on the Fly (60 minutes)

Explain that the mark of an excellent learning facilitator is the ability to adjust on the fly to changing conditions without short-changing the learning process. The most common causes for adjusting on the fly are (a) some unexpected change in time constraints (fire drill, productive tangent, surprise guest speaker, participants working faster or slower than expected, not getting started on time), and (b) a prior assumption or assessment about the learners that's off target (they're more [or less] experienced than you thought, their backgrounds are not what you believed they were, they're more [or less] open to certain types of activities than you expected, and so forth).

Distribute and review Handout 6–35.

Given the main causes for adjusting (time and learner characteristics), there are three principal adjustment factors available to you: learner groupings, logistics of the activity, and activity intensity. The actual adjustments you make involve either "backing off" or "ramping up" the activity in one or more of those three areas.

1. **Learner groupings:** The original plan for grouping learners in an activity is based on the grouping arrangement that will support the greatest amount of learning within the planned time. When reality gets in the way of that, a facilitator can adjust on the fly the number of learner groups working to-

gether, which changes the sizes of the individual groups. The guiding principle is that the more learner groups, the more time and involvement an activity will take. A couple of examples will clarify the use of this strategy. If you've run short on time in an activity planned for pairs or trios of learners, adjust to small groups of five or six instead. There will be fewer groups to report their work, and the overall activity will take less time. Conversely, form more groups or have learners work in pairs or trios if more time has become available. Or, let's consider a situation in which you find that the planned groupings require more or less involvement than the learners are comfortable with. You'll have to adjust the groupings up or down in that situation as well. For example, if the learners are more shy or reserved than you expected, you may need to adjust up to more and smaller groups. If they're more comfortable in large groups and enjoy speaking in front of others, then adjusting down to a few larger groups (or one large group) may be appropriate.

2. **Logistics of the activity:** Adjust the logistics for time or for changing learner needs. When you plan the logistics of an activity ahead of time, it will be much easier to adjust on the fly when you must. Logistics issues include the number of groups (see above), physical layout, conditions in which the learners will work (will they discuss? or first work alone and then discuss? move around or stay in the same place?), results they must produce (report, flipchart, presentation, action), time of day (need to be more physically active later in the day), and learning styles (is there a preponderance of one style?). The guiding principle is this: the more active or complicated the logistics, the more time and active learner involvement the activity will take.

If you've run short on time, one logistics adjustment you can make is backing off the complexity of the logistics. For example, have learners appoint a recorder to take notes in their groups rather than have them draw up flipcharts, or ask groups to report their top three ideas rather than all of the ideas they discussed. Alternatively, instead of having each group provide a complete report, you can use a modified *round robin* approach: each group presents an idea; the following groups only add one idea that's new, and this goes on until all ideas have been presented. The round robin approach reduces redundancy. Conversely, if more time is available, you can ramp up the complexity of your logistics. In these cases, have groups do something physically active (such as build a model, solve a puzzle, or make a flipchart) or have them work on assignments in segments and switch groups between segments.

If you find that the planned logistics will support more (or less) active involvement than is optimal with a particular group of learners, you can adjust the logistics accordingly. Adjust them down for learners who are shy, reserved, novice, sedentary, or at the beginning of a course when they don't know each other; adjust them up for learners who are more extroverted, outgoing, experienced, active in their jobs, and farther along in a course when comfort levels are higher.

3. **Activity intensity:** You can adjust intensity for time issues or learner needs. The more learner centered an activity is, the more "intense" an experience it is for the learners. Intensity of activities ranges from lectures (low intensity) to discussions (moderately low intensity) to structured activities (moderate intensity) to skill practices (high intensity). The guiding principle is that the more intense the activity, the more time it will take, and the more "risk" learners will experience. For example, if you've run short on time, you can turn

down the activity intensity one step (back down from a skill practice on the content to a structured activity, from a structured activity to a discussion, or from a discussion to a lecture).

You may find yourself in a situation in which the planned activity's intensity is not a good match for either the learners' comfort zone or their experience level. Once again, adjust on the fly. You can turn down the intensity (from a skill practice on the content to a structured activity, from a structured activity to a discussion, from a discussion to a lecture). Adjust intensity upward with learners who are beyond the planned intensity in either their comfort zone or experience (ramp up from a lecture to a discussion or from a discussion to a structured activity; ramp up the intensity of a structured activity; or intensify from a structured exercise to a skill practice).

4. **Preparing ahead of time:** The most important aspect of adjusting on the fly is preparing ahead of time. Know which content and activities are most critical, and which are "nice to know." Know which activities reinforce skills and link to application on the job. Analyze your content and activities and identify what you'll adjust (if necessary) and how you'll adjust it. Develop ahead of time the specific changes you'll make in groupings, logistics, or activity intensity, should the need arise. In the classroom, when you make the actual adjustment, it will be seamless in the eyes of your learners—and that's what counts.

Facilitate Learning Activity 5–10.

When learner groups have completed their work, facilitate a debrief discussion according to the questions they were assigned to answer:

◆ **Question:** Which items from the sample module plan in Handout 6–36 are critical, and which are nice to know? If you had to, would you omit any of the activities when adjusting on the fly? Which ones? *Likely answers:*

◆ *Critical:* learning activity on applying learning styles to facilitation of learning activities; debriefing of the learning activity; learning preferences; learning styles

◆ *Nice to know:* the physical learning environment.

◆ **Question:** How would you adjust each activity in Handout 6–36 if you had to? Why? *Likely answers:*

◆ The physical learning environment—show Handout 6–3 and ask if there are questions; answer the questions; move on.

◆ Learning preferences—change interactive lecture on learning preferences to having them read the material and ask questions. Do not adjust whiteboard discussion with three categories (visual, auditory, kinesthetic) and ask learners to volunteer types of activities.

◆ Learning styles—change interactive lecture on learning styles to having them read the material and ask questions.

◆ Learning Activity 5–3—it would be best *not* to adjust this activity because it's the most critical.

◆ Debrief Learning Activity 5–3—show Handout 6–7 and ask if there are questions; answer the questions; move on.

That's adjusting on the fly! You've now mastered the basics of learning facilitation. It's time to begin thinking about application back on the job.

Pass out Handout 6–37. Explain that when you distribute a course evaluation at the very end of a course, the feedback you get is not of high quality because people are anxious to leave. It's a much better strategy to hand out

the evaluation earlier in the session so people can use free time to fill it out. Some facilitators hand it out at the last break, others do so earlier, and some distribute it at the beginning of the course or include it in the first packet of materials the learners receive. Indicate that the participants are to complete the evaluation now or before they leave the program.

3:15   Break (10 minutes)

3:25   Structuring the Development Plan (30 minutes)

It's time to talk about how you'll continue your development beyond our time together. Continuous learning and practice are crucial to individual success. As a facilitator, your role goes beyond this training session. Your role is to make learning happen and to assist in having that learning applied on the job. As the facilitator, you influence the learners for continued development.

People excel in their work by honing their skills and by strengthening major weaknesses. Top performers continually develop themselves. Learners must continue to develop their facilitation competencies. To support this, they should complete the development plan for their continued skill development.

Conduct Learning Activity 5–11, which introduces the learners to a means of planning for their continued competency development. Show slide 3–27 and distribute Handout 6–40. Instruct participants to consult the CD for a blank copy of the Development Plan (without examples).

Note: To support your participants in their learning, refer them to "For Further Reading" at the end of this workbook.

Show slide 3–28. Close the activity by explaining that the best development plans

◆ provide learning experiences that directly support your identified need

♦ take you out of your comfort zone

♦ provide you with a variety of experiences

♦ broaden your perspective.

3:55 Closing the Program (10–20 minutes)

Collect the course evaluations, Handout 6–37. Alternatively, you may request that participants leave the evaluations at their seats or at a designated location. Indicate that the information will be used for continuous improvement of the training.

Thank participants for attending the workshop and for being actively involved in their learning. Encourage them to complete and implement their development plans.

What to Do Next

1. Prepare to deliver the Advanced Facilitation Training two-day course.

2. Review Appendix A: Delivery Preparation Checklist, completing the checklist as a guide for your preparation.

♦ ♦ ♦

The next chapter presents a one-day workshop of facilitation skills, narrowing the focus to facilitating learning experiences.

Slide 3–1

Welcome to Advanced Facilitation Skills Training

Your Name
Date
Location

Slide 3–2

Presenters vs. Facilitators

- In your group:
  - Pick a recorder.
  - Brainstorm differences between presenters and facilitators.
  - Introduce yourselves.
  - Complete the assignment in <u>6 minutes.</u>
  - Present work.

Slide 3–3

How a Facilitator Differs from a Presenter

- Focus is on the learner.
- Shares control with participants.
- Credibility is from the learning environment, not expertise alone.
- Accountability for learning is shared.
- Learners are engaged on multiple levels.

Slide 3–4

Learning Objectives

- Assess one's knowledge and confidence level regarding facilitator competencies, and identify those competencies most in need of development
- Identify participant learning styles and preferences, and implement facilitation techniques to accommodate different styles and preferences
- Analyze various types of learning activities

Slide 3–5

Learning Objectives

- Facilitate a structured bridge activity
- Facilitate a guided discussion
- Develop strategies to facilitate learning while handling the needs of disruptive participants
- Develop strategies to adjust on the fly in a learning event when necessary
- Prepare development plan strategies for facilitation skill practice back on the job

Slide 3–6

Areas of Facilitator Competency

- Credibility
- Creating a learning environment
- Communication skills
- Presentation/facilitation skills
- Instructional strategies
- Use of media

Slide 3–7

Factors in Room Setup

- Number of participants
- Types of learning activities
- Number of teams
- Number of members on each team
- Physical limitations
- Required equipment
- Facilitator's personal space
- Facilitator's delivery style: podium, lectern, or open
- Room temperature
- Peripheral materials and methods
- Refreshments

Slide 3–8

Learning Preferences

- *Visual* - take in and process information through what they see. printed information, pictures, graphics.

- *Auditory* - take in and process information that is heard, including words, alliteration, and song.

- *Kinesthetic* - take in and process information through physical, hands-on experiences.

Slide 3–9

Learning Styles

- Achievers
- Evaluators
- Networkers
- Socializers
- Observers

Slide 3–10

Achievers

- Focus on doing and results
- Are practical
- Like new and challenging experiences
- Solve problems, make decisions, and develop action plans
- Accept the lead role
- Prefer sequence and logical order
- Prefer clear, step-by-step directions
- Are not strongly people oriented
- Take control

Slide 3–11

Evaluators

- Analyze situations
- Use a logical process to resolve issues
- Like detailed questions
- Collect information
- Work within existing guidelines
- Assimilate information and put it into a concise, logical format
- Focus more on theory; less on relationships
- Prefer logically sound, exact, and factual theory

Slide 3–12

Networkers

- Develop close relationships
- Avoid interpersonal conflict
- Use listening skills to develop people networks
- Are more compliant and easily swayed than others
- Avoid risks
- Seek consensus and are slower to make decisions
- Seldom disagree
- Are supportive of others and seek collaboration
- Build trust
- Need direct feedback

Slide 3–13

Socializers

- Like to talk and share
- Enjoy the spotlight and like to have fun
- Prefer to get multiple perspectives
- Good at selling their ideas and building alliances
- Not concerned with details or facts
- Prefer a fast pace and make quick, spontaneous decisions
- In groups, work quickly, seek others' input, persuade others, provide some humor, and volunteer to make the presentation

Slide 3–14

Observers

- View concrete situations from different points of view
- Prefer to observe and conceptualize
- Are reflective thinkers
- Generate many wide-ranging ideas
- Prefer abstract ideas and concepts, not relationships
- Take time to reflect and conceptualize
- Don't like to wing it

Slide 3–15

Instructions

- In your group:
  - Pick a recorder to take notes.
  - Work together to identify ways or techniques to accommodate the learning needs of your assigned learning style.
  - Focus on _how_ each technique addresses the assigned learning style.
  - Pick a presenter.
  - Work for 15 minutes.
- Present your work.

Slide 3–16

Interactive Lecture

- In a traditional lecture:
  - Focus is on the facilitator.
  - Learners are relatively passive.
- To make the lecture interactive:
  - Ask participants questions every few minutes.
  - Invite their questions.
- Use when learners don't know very much about the content.

Slide 3–17

Guided Discussion

- _Definition:_ a discussion/dialogue between facilitator and learners that is guided by a series of planned facilitator questions
- For each learning point to be brought out,
  - Craft a question.
  - Note most likely learner responses.
  - Plan follow-up comments.
- Use when learners know something about the content and can engage it.
- Use this activity to debrief other learning activities.

Slide 3–18

Structured Bridge Activity

- Learners work together.
- Uses content at a deeper level.
- Learners are more active and involved.
- Facilitator's role: organizer, monitor, and guide.
- Used with learners who have some knowledge of the content
- Provides a "bridge" between content and application.

Slide 3–19

Instructions

- In your group:
  - Pick a recorder to take notes.
  - Work together to answer these questions:
    - What is the biggest difference between structured activities and the activities examined so far?
    - Why are these activities called "bridges"?
    - Where do the learners get the content they work with in a structured activity?
    - What are two examples of structured activities?
  - Pick a presenter.
  - Work for 15 minutes.
- Present your work.

Slide 3–20

Instructions

- In your group:
  - Read the case study, Handout 6–11.
  - Work together to answer the case questions.
  - Use Handouts 6–12, 6–13, and 6–14 as reference.
  - You have 30 minutes.
- Present recommendations for learning activities, rationales, and brief activity descriptions.

Slide 3–21

Facilitating Learning Activities Practice Setup

Groups:

- Setting up instructions and monitoring learning activities
- Grouping learners in learning activities
- Sequencing learning activities and giving feedback
- Using media
- Physical presentation

Slide 3–22

Facilitating Learning Activities

Your assignment:

- Design and deliver a structured bridge activity with a guided discussion debrief.
- Maximum length: 10 minutes
- Tomorrow morning
- Resources:
  - Partial handout (you add the rest!)
  - Your observations and experiences
  - Your own experiences and intuition

Slide 3–23

Scenario

You will be facilitating a training course in a hotel. The room is a large rectangular room with a door at one end. Given a group size of 20–24, you will need only about half the room. The design of the course calls for (a) some individual work, (b) some work in pairs, and (c) some small group work.

The grouping of the participants will be changed with each group activity.

There are no breakout rooms.

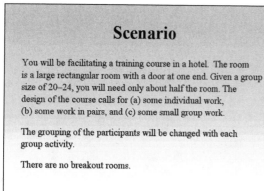

Slide 3–24

Disruptive Participants

- Part 1:
  - Choose a scribe.
  - Identify and describe examples of disruptive participant behavior, and identify and discuss causal factors.
  - Present.
- Part 2:
  - Develop strategies to address disruptive behavior, using Handout 6–31.
  - Present.

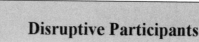

Slide 3–25

Facilitator Tactics

- Not getting caught in one-on-one power struggles
- Using good-natured humor
- Connecting with the participant on a personal level
- Broadening the participation of the rest of the group
- Protecting participants as needed
- Using a separate Issues Chart or Parking Lot to postpone issues
- Recognizing the learner's point and then taking the discussion offline
- Changing the composition of small groups
- Modifying activities or instructional strategies

Slide 3–26

Instructions

- Which items are critical and which are nice to know? If you had to, would you omit any of the activities when adjusting on the fly? If so, which ones?
- How would you adjust each activity? Why?
- Take 20 minutes to make these decisions.
- Be prepared to discuss.

Slide 3–27

Instructions

- Create your development plan.
- Complete and implement the development plan on the job.
- Share your initial plans with another participant.

Slide 3–28

Development Plans

The best development plans will

- provide learning experiences that directly support your identified need
- take you out of your comfort zone
- provide you with diverse experiences
- broaden your perspective.

◆

One-Day Program: Facilitation Skills Training

- ◆ Objectives for facilitating a one-day workshop for learning facilitators

- ◆ Detailed program agenda

- ◆ Comprehensive teaching notes for presenting a one-day training session on facilitation skills

This chapter contains a comprehensive, step-by-step guide for conducting a learning experience for learning facilitators. It is, in essence, "a course within a course," or, to use the more traditional term, a "train-the-trainer" course. This short workshop is focused on helping learners develop and practice learning facilitation skills. The participants will learn specific techniques to conduct and debrief learning activities, ways to manage disruptive participants, methods to manage assessments, and ways to use various forms of media to enhance learning. This workshop provides the opportunity for skill practice with feedback.

This chapter gives you, the workshop facilitator, a listing of all the materials and support requirements, learning activities, and handouts required for a successful delivery.

One-Day Program

LEARNING OBJECTIVES

- ◆ Analyze various types of learning activities.

- ◆ Explain the use of the interactive lecture.

- Facilitate a guided discussion.

- Develop strategies to facilitate learning while handling the needs of disruptive participants.

- Develop strategies to adjust on the fly when necessary in a learning event.

- Prepare development plan strategies for facilitation skill practice back on the job.

MATERIALS

For the facilitator/instructor:

- PowerPoint slide presentation, *One-Day.ppt* (slides 4–1 through 4–16). To access slides for this program, open One-Day.ppt on the accompanying CD. Copies of the slides for this training session are included at the end of this chapter.

- Learning Activity 5–12: Presenters and Facilitators

- Learning Activity 5–13: Skill Practices Case Study

- Learning Activity 5–14: Facilitating Learning Activities Practice Setup

- Learning Activity 5–15: Facilitating Learning Activities Practice

- Learning Activity 5–16: Managing Disruptive Participants

- Learning Activity 5–17: Adjusting on the Fly

- Learning Activity 5–18: Structuring the Development Plan

- wallboard or prepared flipchart—"Parking Lot" (post on a wall prior to beginning the workshop)

- facilitator bio

- projector, screen, and computer for displaying PowerPoint slides; alternatively, overhead transparencies and overhead projector

- flipcharts (two for the facilitator and an appropriate number for participant to share in group exercises)

- blank transparencies

- water-based color markers for facilitator and participants

◆ masking tape

◆ sticky-notes

◆ tent cards

◆ colored paper

◆ scissors.

For the participants:

◆ Handout 6–1: Presenter and Facilitator: What's the Difference?

◆ Handout 6–8: The Interactive Lecture

◆ Handout 6–9: The Guided Discussion

◆ Handout 6–10: The Structured Bridge Activity

◆ Handout 6–11: Facilitation Case Study

◆ Handout 6–12: The Case Study

◆ Handout 6–13: The Role Play

◆ Handout 6–14: The Demonstration and Practice

◆ Handout 6–15: Behavioral Checklist for a Structured Bridge Activity

◆ Handout 6–16: Behavior Checklist for a Guided Discussion

◆ Handout 6–17: Setting Up Instructions and Monitoring Learning Activities (Partial)

◆ Handout 6–18: Grouping Learners in Learning Activities (Partial)

◆ Handout 6–19: Sequencing Learning Activities and Giving Feedback (Partial)

◆ Handout 6–20: Using Media (Partial)

◆ Handout 6–21: Physical Presentation Tips (Partial)

◆ Handout 6–22: Setting Up Instructions and Monitoring Learning Activities (Complete)

◆ Handout 6–23: Grouping Learners in Learning Activities (Complete)

◆ Handout 6–24: Sequencing Learning Activities and Giving Feedback (Complete)

- Handout 6–25: Using Media (Complete)

- Handout 6–26: Physical Presentation Tips (Complete)

- Handout 6–27: Factors for Room Setup (Complete)

- Handout 6–28: Sample Room Layouts

- Handout 6–29: Room Setup Considerations

- Handout 6–30: Tips for Room Setup

- Handout 6–31: Strategies for Dealing with Disruptive Behavior

- Handout 6–32: Recognizing and Responding to Disruptive Learner Behavior

- Handout 6–33: Recommended Strategies to Deal with Disruptive Behaviors

- Handout 6–34: A Comprehensive Response for Dealing with Disruptive Behaviors

- Handout 6–35: Factors in Adjusting on the Fly

- Handout 6–38: Facilitation Training Course Evaluation

- Handout 6–39: Sample Module Plan—Skill Practices Case Study

- Handout 6–40: Structuring the Development Plan

- paper and pens.

USING THE CD

Materials for this training session are provided in this workbook and as electronic files on the accompanying CD. To access the electronic files, insert the CD and click on the appropriate Adobe.pdf or PowerPoint.ppt/.pps document. Further directions and help in locating and using the files can be found in Appendix C: Using the Compact Disc.

You'll note that, although the learning activities for the two-day course are labeled 5–1, 5–2, 5–3, and so on through 5–11, the learning activities for the one-day course begin with 5–12 and continue through 5–18.

AGENDA

8:00 a.m.   Welcome and Introductions (5 minutes)

Have slide 4–1 showing as learners enter the room. Welcome each participant individually.

Introduce yourself *briefly*. Refer to your bio, already in their materials or lying at their tables (see chapter 2) as a source of additional information about you.

Explain that this course is somewhat different from other courses that one might take because it's a "course within a course." All of the methods used to help the learners master facilitation skills are also models of how the methods can be used. Having said that, then, the first technique that will be modeled is beginning a course with an experiential activity so that learners are immediately engaged.

8:05   Presenters and Facilitators (20 minutes)

Conduct Learning Activity 5–12. Distribute Handout 6–1. Using slide 4–2 to reveal activity instructions, conduct this activity, which helps the learners immediately recognize the differences between presenting information and facilitating the actual learning of that information.

In some cases your learners already will know each other, so introductions will not be necessary (pass by that bullet on slide 4–2). When learners don't know each other, this activity is suggested as a way to start that process—allowing learners to introduce themselves in their groups. You can assure them that, as the course continues and they change groups, they'll eventually meet everyone. Many facilitators like to accomplish introductions by having participants introduce themselves one by one. In this case, for example, you might ask them to share a thought on a difference between a presenter and a learning facilitator. This method is not recommended for this course, however, because the course is limited in time.

Learners tend to pay more attention to the time limit in an activity if the time is an unusual number, rather than a multiple of 5—such as 10 minutes, 15 minutes, and so forth.

Show slide 4–3 and debrief the activity.

One hallmark of true facilitation is that, as much as possible, the facilitator doesn't separate herself or himself from the learner audience—she or he is with the learners in the experience all the way. The facilitator is one of them, yet not one of them, and guides them to the learning destination. It's a different role from a teacher/instructor/presenter in a classroom, where there's a clear and obvious separation between the learners and the presenter, and in which the presenter is positioned as an expert who knows all while the learners are passive recipients of the knowledge. Certainly, the facilitator knows the subject area. But more than that, the facilitator is concerned with helping the learners know and apply the subject matter. The facilitator's goal is not simply to inform, but also to equip the learners for self-development and growth, for continual learning about the subject to the point of mastery.

There are five main characteristics that differentiate facilitators from presenters:

1. *The facilitator keeps the focus on the learner.* When you observe both a presentation and a facilitated learning event, many obvious differences appear. One of the most important differences, however, is one that is not visible: the *focus*. In a presentation, the focus is on the presenter. All of the materials, the presenter's behaviors, and the actions are centered on the presenter. The goals for the presentation are to cover the material, and to showcase the presenter's expertise and skill. Conversely, in a facilitated learning event the focus is on the learner. All of the materials, the facilitator's behaviors, and the activities are centered on helping learners learn and apply the content. The goal here is simple and profound: make the learning and application happen.

2. *Facilitators share control.* A presenter presents information or content to the audience. A good presen-

ter has excellent command of language and vocabulary, an engaging speaking style, and a command of the subject. By definition, an excellent presentation results in the audience being informed about the subject matter and taking away useful information. Because the presentation centers on the presenter, that person is in control of the subject and how the audience engages with the subject (or not). The presenter decides when questions are allowed, and which questions to address. Most of the action is on the part of the presenter; the audience remains largely passive. By exercising this control, the presenter takes on full responsibility for the audience's increase in knowledge—or not. The presenter has no guarantee that the listeners will use the information or learn from it.

Effective learning facilitation, however, only *begins* with content expertise and presentation skills. An effective facilitator gives up much of the control of the content to the learner audience, and shares responsibility for the learning with them. The facilitator establishes the climate, learning structure, and flow of the learning. The learners have a great deal of flexibility in asking and responding to questions, engaging the facilitator and peer learners in discussion, and applying the content to their jobs.

3. *Facilitators derive credibility from more than subject matter expertise.* A presenter gains (or loses) her or his credibility in the minds of the audience based on the content of the presentation, on her or his mastery of that content, and on relating the content to learners' relevant experience. The presenter's ability to give examples, tell "war stories," and answer questions from a strong background and experience results in "expert" credibility. When a presenter doesn't know the answer to a question, or when the presenter's answer and the learner's experiences aren't in sync, credibility in the eyes of the audience is damaged or disappears altogether.

Whereas content expertise and control provide credibility for presenters, what facilitators *do* with these components is what creates credibility for them. Facilitator credibility is derived from

- creating and sustaining a supportive learning environment

- linking the learning to the learners' jobs

- keeping the spotlight on the learners

- being flexible and adjusting the content to the learners' needs in the moment

- helping learners "self-discover" the learning.

When the facilitator is (rarely, of course!) asked a question that he or she can't answer, the facilitator helps the group find the answer together and, by doing so, retains and even increases credibility. Alternatively, if the facilitator doesn't know the answer, but has the confidence to say, "I don't know, but I'll find out," it will not damage credibility.

4. *Accountability for learning is shared.* The learners have a great deal of flexibility in asking and responding to questions, engaging the facilitator and their peer learners in discussion, and applying the content to their jobs. Because control is jointly held, accountability for learning also is joint. Not being passive, the learners are accountable both to learn and to apply the content as the facilitator guides the learning and application.

5. *Learning happens at multiple levels.* As the learners gain more control, the facilitator builds on the learners' experiences engaging with and applying the content. Whereas presentation occurs at the thinking level, facilitation occurs at multiple levels: thinking, feeling, intuitive, physical, synergistic, and emotional. The facilitator must respond to, keep track of, and invite learner involvement at all

of these levels as the learning event proceeds. And the paradox is this: the more control that's given to the learners, the more real learning occurs.

When groups share their work, "round-robin" style is strongly suggested. In this method, one group shares one item that they discussed, then the next group shares one item, then the next group, and so on. Learners can be instructed to share another of their items if a previous group shared one it already had, or they can add special emphasis to an item (and the facilitator places an extra checkmark next to the item on the chart). If there are multiple items to share (for example, if the groups were asked to answer three questions), share answers to each question by starting with a different group each time so different groups get to be first. Doing so produces the following results:

- *All learners remain participants throughout the sharing of information because each group doesn't have to wait long to share.*

- *All learners feel that their information is given equal importance.*

- *All learners feel that they had important information to share; when one group shares all its information before moving on to the next group, the last groups to share often have no new contributions to make. They feel their participation wasn't important and the other groups "stole their thunder."*

8:25   Complete Course Introduction (5 minutes)

Share information about the course schedule, facilities, and any other "housekeeping" issues.

Show slides 4–4 and 4–5. Ask for a show of hands regarding which objectives are the most desired by the group. This will give you a sense of what material can be handled more quickly and which sections will need more time. Your emphasis will differ each time you facilitate this workshop because it's always based on the learners' stated needs.

Explain that there is a lot of content and application to experience during this day together. To accomplish all of it, it's necessary to establish some ground rules.

Reveal slide 4–6. Explain that these are proposed group norms, standard operating procedures, or principles that will help everyone work together to make this a great learning experience. Ask learners for their agreement on the ground rules.

Refer to your pre-posted wallchart titled "Parking Lot." It can be a sketch or a graphic image of a parking lot with three rows of spaces, labeled "Short-term," "Long-term," and "Valet." Explain that the parking lot is the place for participants to "park" questions until a more appropriate time to answer them. Indicate that the participants are to use the sticky-notes to write their questions and place them in the appropriate column on the chart: short-term = I need an answer today, long-term = I need an answer sometime during the training program, and valet = I need an answer in the near future after the course is finished.

We suggest that you gather and address the sticky-notes after breaks or at the end of the day. Address each note by answering the question, or by explaining when and how you will answer the question.

8:30   Facilitation techniques: The Interactive Lecture Learning Activity (20 minutes)

Distribute Handout 6–8 and display slide 4–7. For the next 10 minutes, conduct an interactive lecture about the **interactive lecture** activity. Throughout the activity, pause and ask the learners questions and invite their questions as well. You may use the following questions at intervals as you deliver the content (the actual content from which you'll draw follows these suggested questions):

♦ Who has experienced a lecture in the past?

♦ What are the pros and cons of a lecture as a learning activity?

♦ Why would we want learner participation during a lecture?

♦ How would you add the "interactive" element to this activity?

- In what types of situations should the interactive lecture be used?

The foundation of all skills is knowledge, and learners must know before they do. The traditional lecture applies to learners who don't have any (or have very little) background in the content of the lesson or course. It's an activity characterized by relative passivity on the part of the participants (they're usually listening, reading, or observing without interacting; by more focus on the facilitator (who must deliver the content because participants don't know it); and (usually) by individual rather than group work.

It's important to make a lecture interactive—hence the name. Even learners who know very little about the content can respond to questions that engage them at a level they can understand and that relate to their own experiences.

To make a lecture interactive, the facilitator presents content (a mini-lecture of a few minutes), and then invites participation by asking the learners questions and by inviting their questions. The facilitator continues to share content and invite participation throughout the entire activity. By inviting participation, what is normally thought of as a lecture *by* the facilitator becomes an interactive lecture *with* the learners. This activity should be used when learners know relatively little about the content, and therefore must learn about it before they can interact with it.

Here are some tips for using this activity:

- Plan the intervals at which you might ask the participants if they have questions.

- Plan a couple of your key questions intended to gain participation.

- Never deliver a "straight lecture" for more than 10–15 minutes without inviting participation in some way.

Interactive lecture is part of a category of learning activities that focus on disseminating content, and in which learners are relatively passive. Other such activities include

◆ reading books, handouts

◆ watching videos/films; viewing PowerPoint presentations, slides, overhead transparencies

◆ completing pre-work

◆ taking notes

◆ completing self-assessments, such as checklists and quizzes.

The same principles for creating interaction and engagement can be used during facilitation of those activities.

8:50 Facilitation techniques: The Guided Discussion Learning Activity (20 minutes)

Show slide 4–8 and distribute Handout 6–9. Conduct the following **guided discussion** about guided discussions.

Remember that a guided discussion is a planned discussion in which the facilitator prepares questions that will guide learners into "discovery" of the learning points. The facilitator asks specific, planned questions to draw learning points from the learners. You augment their responses by making more in-depth learning points.

Guided discussion question: What comes to your mind when you hear the term *guided discussion*?

◆ *Likely learner response:* Facilitator is guiding participants in a certain direction.

◆ *Augmenting comment:* Yes, that's right, and it's done with open-ended questions.

Guided discussion question: What do you think is the difference between an interactive lecture and a guided discussion?

◆ *Likely learner response:* In an interactive lecture, most of the content still comes from the facilitator. In a guided discussion, it's more even.

◆ *Augmenting comment:* Correct. There is more learner engagement in a guided discussion. And questions are preplanned and matched to specific learning points, rather than simply interjected on the fly as they are in the interactive lecture.

Guided discussion question: Why do you think learners can be more engaged in a guided discussion than in the previous type of activity?

◆ *Likely learner response:* They know more about the content, so they can participate more.

◆ *Augmenting comment:* So, the facilitator has to do a good job ahead of time in determining how much the learners know so the guided discussion can be chosen in the right situation.

Guided discussion question: How does a facilitator "do" a guided discussion?

◆ *Likely learner response:* Plans questions ahead of time.

◆ *Augmenting comment:* Not only the questions—the facilitator also plans on what the learners' most likely responses are, and on what augmenting content the facilitator will add.

Guided discussion question: Can you think of any time, other than when disseminating content, that a facilitator might use a guided discussion?

◆ *Likely learner response:* ???? (probably won't have an answer)

◆ *Augmenting comment:* A special type of guided discussion is called a **debriefing,** and it's used after a learning activity to help the learners process what happened and what they learned. It's designed to close the gaps in the learning, to summarize the main points, and to help the learners apply the content to the job. Here are a couple typical sets of debriefing questions: What happened in the activity? How did that make you feel? What principles or generalizations can you infer from it? How will you apply it going forward? What went well? What could have been done better? How does this apply to your job? What will you do differently in the future?

Now that we've looked at two ways to disseminate content with increased interaction, after the break we'll take a look at the more interactive learner-centered activities.

9:10   Break (10 minutes)

9:20   The Structured Bridge Learning Activity (20 minutes)

Show slide 4–9. Take a few minutes to explain that the learners in structured activities work together to understand and use content at a deeper level than simple comprehension—at levels such as synthesis, integration, evaluation, and application. Learners are more active and involved than in interactive lectures or guided discussions. The focus is on the learners, and the facilitator's role is that of organizer, monitor, and guide. These activities are used with learners who have some knowledge of the desired content and who are ready for more depth and concept application.

Distribute Handout 6–10 and conduct a guided discussion, using the handout and slide 4–9 for reference.

Notes: As practice for *you*, we suggest that you develop "learners' most likely responses" and "augmenting content" for each of the following guided discussion questions that you use. Do that for all remaining guided discussions in the course.

You'll notice that this activity is not the same as in the two-day course outlined in chapter 3. There you actually facilitate a structured bridge activity about structured bridge activities. That's a highly recommended recursive method. In the one-day course, however, time won't allow a full-blown structured activity, so a guided discus-

sion is recommended. (This is a good example of how to adjust for time by backing down an activity, as discussed later.)

Suggested guided discussion questions:

- How much do learners know about the content when they're participating in a structured bridge activity?

- What will they do with that content during the activity?

- How involved are the learners in this type of activity, compared with their involvement in a guided discussion or interactive lecture?

- What's the facilitator's role in this activity?

- Why are these activities called "bridges" between content and practice?

If the following points haven't been made by the learners, include them in the discussion:

- To support the activity, content sometimes has been acquired earlier in the same course. In other instances, the learners have the content and experience when they walk in. In the latter case, the first type of exercise used is often a structured activity. The learner groups are given questions to answer or a problem to solve; in the process of doing so, they discover the new content.

- Often the activity is conducted before the content is revealed so the learners have the "first crack" at discovering the content within their own knowledge base. The content is then presented in a debriefing guided discussion to ensure all the points have been made.

Explain other types of structured bridge activities, such as these:

- **Solo work:** learners are given an assignment to work on alone (such as to fill out a questionnaire or analyze a problem); then they discuss it with others.

◆ **Small group discussion:** small groups of learners are given a topic to discuss or questions to answer; they work together, and then present their results.

◆ **Group inquiry:** the learners are provided with content, and they work together to identify questions they have about that content.

◆ **Information search:** learners are given reference materials and must search through them for answers to questions presented by the facilitator. In a blended learning experience (in which face-to-face learning and e-learning are combined), the process may involve using the Internet to conduct searches or to download information.

◆ **Small group assignment/problem solving:** small groups of learners are given a problem to solve, a situation to analyze, a list of principles or guidelines to develop in response to a problem, and so forth.

◆ **Peer teaching:** small groups of learners study the material, then teach it to the other participants or groups in the class. Determining the teaching methodology is part of the activity, and it's left up to the groups.

◆ **Games ("Jeopardy," "Bingo," "Concentration"):** a version of a popular game can be developed to assist learners in comprehending, remembering, and applying content that has been presented.

The "how to" section for structured bridge activities mentions forming learner groups and monitoring the work of learner groups. If the participants ask questions about how to do that, tell them that it will be covered in a later activity.

9:40   Advanced Structured Activities (Skill Practices) (70 minutes, including a 10-minute break when convenient)

Explain that once the learners have mastered knowledge and applied it at a deeper level in a bridge activity, the next part of the learning is skill practice. This is exactly what it says—the actual practice of the skill. If the skill is driving a car, then the skill practice is actually driving a car (or a simulator). If the skill is conducting a job interview or making a sales presentation, then the skill practice is conducting a mock interview or sales presentation. If the skill is analyzing a situation and making recommendations, then the skill practice is analyzing a case situation and making recommendations. In other words, **skill practice** is the performance of the skill, adjusted when necessary for the learning environment.

You're now going to learn about skill practices by participating in one.

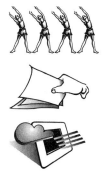

Conduct Learning Activity 5–13. Distribute Handouts 6–11, 6–12, 6–13, and 6–14. Review the activity directions on slide 4–10.

Conduct the presentations and debriefings in the following manner. For each type of learning activity (case, role play, demonstration and practice):

1. Have the small group make its presentation.

2. Conduct a debriefing guided discussion to share learning points that may have been missed in the presentation and to emphasize critical points (see below for each activity's learning points).

3. Review the handout that accompanies the activity (6–12 for case studies, 6–13 for role play, and 6–14 for demonstration and practice).

4. Answer any questions that remain.

Here are learning points for the case study on driving etiquette:

1. How would John set this up? What skill is this? What materials would he use? [This is a mental skill—deciding what to do in an etiquette-related

situation. Case study, presenting problem situations, is the appropriate activity. It needs to be set up so that the learners must make etiquette decisions in situations. John would set this up as learners working together— partners, small groups, and so on. For materials, John would write the etiquette situations for which the learners must decide what to do.]

2. What would he have the learners do as part of the case study activity? [He could make small groups, assign each one a situation, and ask them to identify what they should do in each scenario. He has two needs to fill in this activity: have the learners actually practice the skill—that is, make etiquette decisions—and have them work together to share ideas.]

3. What potential pitfalls should he watch out for as he facilitates the activity? Why? [The situations need to be realistic and not too simple. He could even develop specific questions for each scenario that the learners could answer to make it more challenging and to provoke them to analyze the skill at an even deeper level. The group sizes should be in tune with the learners' comfort levels—that is, smaller groups if the learners are still new to each other, larger groups if they are more comfortable.]

4. How will he measure the learners' success in solving the case? [The course content on etiquette would include criteria for what a good etiquette decision "looks like." For example, a good etiquette decision (a) takes all parties' needs into account, (b) is based on "rules of the road" that are commonly known, and (c) realizes when to "give" even if one is right, and so on. The criteria would be used to examine each small group's answers to the scenarios.]

Here are the learning points for the role play on resolving a fender-bender:

1. How would John set this up? What skill is this? What materials would he use? [This is an interpersonal skill—interacting with another person. Role play is the appropriate activity. For materials, John would write up the scenarios according to his decision about type of role play (see below); that is, he could develop a script for the learners to read in the role play; or give them the outline of a scenario, and let them run with it.]

2. What types of role play should he consider? [John would have to make a decision as to what kind of role play should be facilitated, on a continuum from less challenging to more challenging. Factors that might influence his decision include how difficult the learners have found the content to this point—that is, the harder the content is for them, the simpler the role play; the group's comfort level with role play activities—that is, the less comfort, the simpler the role play; and whether this particular skill is process oriented with certain steps that must be followed to have a successful conversation (would lead to a more scripted role play), or is product oriented with many ways the conversation can be implemented as long as a specific result is achieved (would lead to a more improvised role play).]

3. What factors will be important for him to consider? [Learners' comfort level with role play activities; time available; number of learners; whether learners will receive feedback from the facilitator or from each other; and complexity of the content.]

4. How will he measure the learners' success in enacting the role play? [John has two choices in measurement, and it depends on how the content is taught in the course: (a) if the course content implies that this skill is process oriented, then the measure would be a checklist of behavioral steps

that can be checked off by an observer; (b) if the course content implies that this skill is product oriented, then the measure would be a checklist of criteria for a "good" fender-bender conversation that could be checked off by an observer.]

Here is a list of learning points for the demonstration and practice on driving in foggy conditions:

1. How would John set this up? What skill is this? What materials/tools would he use? [John would have two choices here, depending on the experience level of the learners: (a) if they are very inexperienced in driving, he might use a simpler wheeled vehicle, such as a scooter, to demonstrate what happens to traction in foggy conditions, and the principles of handling the foggy environment, before having them practice in a real car; (b) if they are more experienced, he might use a real car in an empty parking lot to demonstrate with an opaque shield over the window to suggest foggy visibility.]

2. What would he have the learners do as part of the practice? [They would observe him as he showed them what to do. Then they would do it themselves.]

3. How will he measure the learners' success in the practice segment? [An observer using a checklist of steps to follow would observe, check off items, and give learners feedback as they practice the skill. John would have to make a decision regarding whether he, as the facilitator, must give the feedback or if the learners can give feedback to each other. With a behavioral checklist, it's relatively easy for learners to give each other feedback. Sometimes, however, it's a better fit with organization culture for the facilitator to give the feedback to each learner.]

 Explain that the learners will now have the opportunity to facilitate an activity (a guided discussion) themselves, and that the setup for this skill practice is next.

10:50   Planning Learning Activities (20 minutes)

Facilitate Learning Activity 5–14.

Learning Activity 5–14 instructs you to divide the learners into five groups. These groups should be approximately equal in size. Learners can count off to be assigned to groups randomly, or they can choose that topic on which they're most interested in working.

11:10   Preparation Time (50 minutes)

After the activity has been set up, tell the learners that they will now have a "lab" during which they can design and prepare for their guided discussions. Explain that you'll be in the room to answer questions and make suggestions if they get stuck. Tell them that the lab is scheduled for 50 minutes, until lunch. Lunch will be from noon until 1:00, at which time the presentations will begin. Offer the option of shortening lunch to have more lab time.

It's a nice touch to have various media available for learners to use in designing their activities and materials (such as colored paper, markers, blank transparencies, scissors, and tape). Let them know that the quality of their materials won't matter—it's the thought and designs that will.

Learners likely will be concerned about the "partial" handouts (6–17 through 6–21) about their perceived inability to deliver a good guided discussion in seven minutes. Here are some suggested responses:

◆ The partial handouts are meant to give you a head start on the information you might choose to deliver in your activities. You have a lot of knowledge and experience that will add to the handouts.

◆ Complete handouts will be distributed when the activity is over.

◆ You'll have to limit to two or three the number of learning points that you'll cover.

> ♦ This is a microcosm of real-world application; we never have enough time to deliver the content we would like to include.

Noon   Lunch (60 minutes)

1:00 p.m.   Facilitating Learning Activities Practice (110 minutes, including a 10-minute break when convenient)

Facilitate Learning Activity 5–15.

This activity is recursive in two ways: (a) the learners are learning the skill of guided discussion by actually practicing it, and (b) they're learning about other aspects of facilitation (such as setting up and structuring learning activities, grouping learners in learning activities, pacing and monitoring learning activities, using media, performing physical presentation) by participating in activities about that content.

This activity is planned to take 110 minutes: 20 minutes each for five group facilitations. Plan to take a 10-minute break at a suitable point during this time span (for example, 2:15 p.m.), bringing the total time for the activity to two hours and 15 minutes.

Here are suggested guided questions for use in debriefing:

- ♦ What went well in *developing* the guided discussion?

  - ♦ What were your biggest challenges in *developing* the guided discussion? How did you overcome them?

  - ♦ What would you do differently the next time?

  - ♦ What general principles can you infer about *developing* a guided discussion?

- ♦ What went well in *facilitating* the guided discussion?

  - ♦ What were your biggest challenges in *facilitating* the guided discussion? How did you overcome them?

  - ♦ What would you do differently the next time?

- ◆ What general principles can you infer about *facilitating* a guided discussion?

- ◆ What was new information for you regarding setting up and structuring learning activities?

  - ◆ What will you do differently going forward?

- ◆ What was new information for you regarding grouping learners in learning activities?

  - ◆ What will you do differently going forward?

- ◆ What was new information for you regarding pacing and monitoring learning activities?

  - ◆ What will you do differently going forward?

- ◆ What was new information for you regarding using media?

  - ◆ What will you do differently going forward?

- ◆ What was new information for you regarding physical presentation?

  - ◆ What will you do differently going forward?

Because many of your learners' answers to these questions will be specific to their experience, "go with the flow" as you augment their responses and continue the activity. However, common themes to expect in their answers (or for you to make sure are brought out) include the following:

- ◆ *Facilitation is harder than it looks.*

- ◆ *It's a good thing to have models and methods to follow so you don't have to reinvent the wheel each time.*

- ◆ *Facilitation is multilayered; many aspects come together to support the learning in the moment.*

- ◆ *The facilitator's focus is on all the layers of what is happening at the time; an apt analogy is the director of a play.*

Refer to the document titled "Facilitation Guidelines," on the accomanying CD, for tips to enhance facilitation skills.

Mention to the learners that during the various activities they've probably noticed how room and seating arrange-

ments affect learning. Explain that this will be the focus now.

2:50   Room and Seating Setup (20 minutes)

Reveal slide 4–13 and conduct a guided discussion on how the room might be set up in the scenario.

Here are some suggested guided discussion questions:

◆ Where should the door be?

◆ How should the facilitator's area (table, materials, audiovisual equipment, screen) be arranged?

◆ What type of seating arrangement should be used for individual work?

◆ What type of seating arrangement should be used for pairs work?

◆ What type of seating arrangement should be used for small group work?

During the guided discussion, ensure that their answers include the basics, such as

◆ a front table for the facilitator's guide, media, and projector. Depending on the media support, the projector may be a computer projection system with the media on a CD, or it may be an overhead projector with transparencies of PowerPoint slides. In either case, the projector could be on a cart inside the "U" or on the facilitator's table.

◆ a door at the back of the room.

◆ no podium.

◆ a side table for handouts and program materials.

◆ a screen behind and just to the side of the facilitator's table.

◆ a table for refreshments, against a wall and behind the seating.

A U-style setup will enable participants to interact, the facilitator to move among the participants, individual work to be done, and pairs to work together.

Even if you had an activity with a group of three people, two could remain seated and the third could move a chair inside the U to face the other two. Because the design of the course calls for (a) some individual work, (b) working in pairs, and (c) some small group work, the U shape allows for interaction and pairs, while team work can be accomplished with the team tables in the back.

Refer to "Media Checklist," on the accompanying CD, and position it as a job aid to ensure that the facilitator has considered all the implications of the media.

The remaining issue is to allow for larger group work. Because the room is larger than needed, place team tables in the back of the room. This provides a place for the larger groups to meet and conduct their group activities, and includes the advantage of not having "dead space" in the room that hinders group cohesiveness. Given the size of the room, there should be enough wall space by the team tables for posting of group work.

Close this section by distributing Handouts 6–27, 6–28, 6–29, and 6–30, explaining that these are tips to help ensure that the environment enhances learning.

Now that we've looked at many important factors that influence learning effectiveness, we'll take a look at two more critical factors: managing the disruptive participant and adjusting on the fly.

3:10   Managing Disruptive Participants (20 minutes)

Explain that there are several types of learners in any learning environment, including

- people who wish to learn and are there voluntarily

- those who want to hone a skill or pick up new ideas

- people sent by their managers

◆ those who are simply taking a break from the daily grind.

No matter which group participants belong to, they're all trying to fulfill their needs and agendas. Some of these needs and agendas are related to the learning, and some are not. When participants act to fulfill a non-learning-related need, we tend to label them "difficult" because their behavior can disrupt the learning for themselves and others. Disruptive behavior occurs when a participant acts according to his or her individual needs or agenda and, as a result, the learning of other participants is minimized.

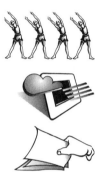

Facilitate Learning Activity 5–16. Use slide 4–14 to display the instructions for the activity, and use Handout 6–31 as directed.

Here are some answers you can expect when the learners describe typical disruptive behavior (be sure to make some of these points if they don't):

◆ engaging in side conversation

◆ talking too much, monopolizing discussion

◆ complaining, being negative about the class or the organization

◆ daydreaming, not really being "in the class"

◆ heckling the facilitator

◆ challenging the facilitator on content or technique, being a "know-it-all"

◆ telling jokes or clowning around at inappropriate times

◆ making an inappropriate remark (sexist, racist, and such)

- doing other work, reading the newspaper, or making/taking cell phone calls

- remaining silent, not participating verbally

- withdrawing from the group interpersonally, physically, or both

- going off on a tangent, missing the point.

Conduct a debrief discussion using Handouts 6–31 and 6–32. Here are some of the most likely causes for those behaviors (that is, the learner's personal agenda):

- learner is bored

- learner is not engaged in the work

- learner is distracted by external matters

- learner is unhappy about the organization and is using the class as an opportunity to vent

- learner wants attention, the spotlight

- learner wants to be acknowledged for expertise

- learner is uncomfortable with the subject matter

- learner is shy, reserved.

The underlying causal factor for most disruptive behavior is that the participant has a personal agenda she or he is supporting. Why do some people end up labeled as disruptive participants? For example, say that a participant challenges your expertise in front of the class because of his or her personal agenda of wanting to be acknowledged for his or her expertise. This behavior is not directed at you, and it's not about you—but it feels like it is!

In that situation, it's very easy for you to react personally. A personal agenda arises on your part, which might be to prove your own expertise and avoid damaging (or possibly even enhance) your own credibility in front of the class. So, a behavior arises out of your own personal agenda, and you get into a debate with the participant. Who wins? No one!

Your response to difficult behavior must be depersonalized. To begin, rather than label people "difficult participants," call it "disruptive behavior." In this way, you're labeling the behavior—not the person. Then, your actions must focus always on helping the learning occur. To do that, you must strive to meet that person's agenda. Counterintuitive as that feels, it's usually true that when you meet that person's agenda, the agenda goes away, and the disruptive behavior is extinguished.

After the groups have presented and their items have been discussed, conduct the following interactive lecture to round out the learning points.

Complete Learning Activity 5–16 to develop the strategies for addressing disruptive behavior. Review its depiction of what must happen in a facilitator's thought processes when disruptive behavior occurs.

Show slide 4–15 and debrief the activity using Handout 6–33.

In general, facilitator tactics for handling disruptive behavior should include

- not getting caught in one-on-one power struggles

- using good-natured humor

- connecting with the participant on a personal level

- broadening the participation of the rest of the group

- protecting participants as needed

- using a separate "Issues Chart" or a "Parking Lot" to postpone issues until they are appropriate for discussion

- recognizing the learner's point and then taking the discussion off-line during breaks, lunches, and at the end of the day

- changing the small group composition

- modifying activities or instructional strategies.

Distribute Handout 6–34, which integrates the disruptive behavior with participant and facilitator agendas and facilitator response. Instruct the participants to use this handout as reference material.

Pass out Handout 6–37. Explain that when you distribute a course evaluation at the very end of a course, the feedback you get is not of high quality because people are anxious to leave. It's a much better strategy to hand out the evaluation earlier in the session so people can complete it during free time. Some facilitators hand it out at the last break, others hand it out earlier, and some even include it in the materials distributed at the beginning of the course or include it in the first packet of materials the learners receive. Ask your learners to fill out the evaluation before the end of the workshop.

3:30   Break (10 minutes)

3:40   Adjusting on the Fly (30 minutes)

There are many things that can get a learning event off track from a schedule standpoint. Participant behavior is only one factor. Sometimes activities take longer than planned, or learners don't return from lunch or breaks on time, or you got started a little later than you intended. Whatever the reason, there are times when you'll need to make adjustments to get back on schedule. This section—Adjusting on the Fly—is designed to help you do that.

Explain that the mark of an excellent learning facilitator is the ability to adjust on the fly to changing conditions without short-changing the learning process. The most common causes for adjusting on the fly are (a) unexpected change in time constraints (fire drill, productive tangent, surprise guest speaker, participants working faster or slower than expected, delay in starting), and (b) a prior assumption or assessment about the learners is off target (they're more [or less] experienced than you thought, their backgrounds aren't what you believed they were, they're more [or less] open to certain types of activities than you expected, and so forth).

Distribute Handout 6–35 and review its contents.

Given the main causes for adjusting (time and learner characteristics), there are three principal adjustment factors available to you: learner groupings, logistics of the activity, and activity intensity. The actual adjustments you make involve either "backing off" or "ramping up" the activity in one or more of those three areas:

1. **Learner groupings:** The original plan for grouping learners in an activity is based on the grouping arrangement that will support the greatest amount of learning within the planned time. When reality gets in the way of that, a facilitator can adjust on the fly the number of learner groups working together, which changes the sizes of the individual groups. The guiding principle is that the more learner groups, the more time and involvement an activity will take. A couple of examples will clarify the use of this strategy. If you've run short on time in an activity planned for pairs or trios of learners, adjust to small groups of five or six instead. There will be fewer groups to report their work, and the overall activity will take less time. Conversely, form more groups or have learners work in pairs or trios if more time has become available. Or, let's consider a situation in which you find that the planned groupings require more or less involvement than the learners are comfortable with. You'll have to adjust the groupings up or down in that situation as

well. For example, if the learners are more shy or reserved than you expected, you may need to adjust up to more and smaller groups. If they're more comfortable in large groups and enjoy speaking in front of others, then adjusting down to a few larger groups (or one large group) may be appropriate.

2. **Logistics of the activity:** Adjust the logistics for time or for changing learner needs. When you plan the logistics of an activity ahead of time, it will be much easier to adjust on the fly when you must. Logistics issues include the number of groups (see above), physical layout, conditions in which the learners will work (will they discuss? or first work alone and then discuss? move around or stay in the same place?), results they must produce (report, flipchart, presentation, action), time of day (need to be more physically active later in the day), and learning styles (is there a preponderance of one style?). The guiding principle is this: the more active and complicated the logistics, the more time and active learner involvement the activity will take.

   If you've run short on time, one logistics adjustment you can make is backing off the complexity of the logistics. For example, have learners appoint a recorder to take notes in their groups rather than have them draw up flipcharts, or ask groups to report their top three ideas rather than all of the ideas they discussed. Alternatively, instead of having each group provide a complete report, you can use a modified *round-robin* approach: each group presents an idea; the following groups only add one idea that's new, and this goes on until all ideas have been presented. The round robin approach reduces redundancy. Conversely, if more time is available, you can ramp up the complexity of your logistics: have groups do something physically active, such as build a model, solve a puzzle, or make a flipchart; or instruct them to work on assignments in segments and then switch groups between segments.

If you find that the planned logistics will support more (or less) active involvement than is optimal with a particular group of learners, you can adjust the logistics accordingly. Back them off for learners who are shy, reserved, novice, sedentary, or at the beginning of a course when they don't know each other; and you can ramp up the logistics for learners who are more extroverted, outgoing, experienced, active in their jobs, and farther along in a course when comfort levels are higher.

3. **Activity intensity:** You can adjust intensity for time issues or learner needs. The more learner centered an activity, the more "intense" an experience it is for the learners. Intensity of activities ranges from lectures (low intensity) to discussions (moderately low intensity) to structured activities (moderate intensity) to skill practices (high intensity). The guiding principle is that the more intense the activity, the more time it will take, and the more "risk" learners will experience. For example, if you've run short on time, you can turn down the activity intensity one step (back down from a skill practice on the content to a structured activity, from a structured activity to a discussion, or from a discussion to a lecture).

You may find yourself in a situation in which the planned activity's intensity is not a good match for either the learners' comfort zone or their experience level. Once again, adjust on the fly. You can turn down the intensity (from a skill practice on the content to a structured activity, from a structured activity to a discussion, from a discussion to a lecture). Adjust intensity upward with learners who are beyond the planned intensity in either their comfort zone or experience (ramp up from a lecture to a discussion or from a discussion to a structured activity; ramp up the intensity of a structured activity; or intensify from a structured exercise to a skill practice).

The most important aspect of adjusting on the fly is preparing ahead of time. Know which content and activities are most critical, and which are "nice to know." Know which activities reinforce skills and link to application on the job. Analyze your content and activities and identify what you'll adjust (if necessary) and how you'll adjust it. Develop ahead of time the specific changes you'll make in groupings, logistics, or activity intensity, should the need arise. In the classroom, making the actual adjustment will be seamless in the eyes of your learners—and that's what counts.

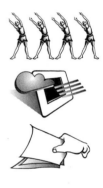

Facilitate Learning Activity 5–17, using slide 4–16 and Handout 6–39.

When learner groups have completed their work, facilitate a debrief discussion according to the questions they were assigned to answer:

♦ **Question:** Which items from the sample module plan in Handout 6–39 are critical and which are nice to know? If you had to, would you omit any of the activities when adjusting on the fly? Which ones? *Answers to expect from learners:*

♦ *Critical:* group presentations and accompanying debriefs

♦ *Nice to know:* ending debrief discussion.

♦ **Question:** How would you adjust each activity in Handout 6–39 if you had to? Why? *Answers to expect from learners:*

♦ Introduction—cut content to 5 minutes rather than 10.

- Case study work—give learners the first answers (or if really short of time, even the first two answers) to each set of case questions so they won't have to work as long.

- Group presentations—when doing a round robin, have each group share only one item and stop after two rounds.

- Short debrief after each presentation—keep it the same.

- Final large group debriefing—cut to 5 minutes rather than 10.

That's adjusting on the fly! You've now mastered the basics of learning facilitation. It's time to begin thinking about application back on the job.

4:10   Structuring the Development Plan (30 minutes)

Continuous learning and practice are crucial to individual success. As a facilitator, your role goes beyond this training session. Your role is to make learning happen and to assist in having that learning applied on the job. As the facilitator, you influence the learners for continued development.

People excel in their work by honing their skills and by strengthening major weaknesses. Top performers continually develop themselves. Learners must continue to develop their facilitation competencies. To support this, they should complete the development plan for their continued skill development.

Conduct Learning Activity 5–18, which introduces the learners to structuring an action plan for continued competency development.

Pass out Handout 6–40. It presents an action plan worksheet, with one sample entry supplied, so you can continue your progress toward excellence in facilitation. Indicate that a blank form with no sample entry is presented on the accompanying CD.

Allow approximately 20 minutes of individual work for learners to get started on their development plans. Instruct participants to consult the CD for a bland Development Plan (without examples).

Note: To support your participants in their learning, refer them to the "For Further Reading" section at the back of this workbook.

When time is up, close the activity by indicating that the best development plans

- provide learning experiences that directly support your identified need

- take you out of your comfort zone

- provide you with a variety of experiences

- broaden your perspective.

4:40   Closing the Program (20 minutes)

Collect the course evaluations, Handout 6–37. Alternatively, you may request that participants leave the evaluations at their seats or at a designated location. Indicate that the information will be used for continuous improvement of the training.

Explain that they still have some steps to accomplish before this learning experience is complete. They are to

1. prepare to deliver the Facilitation Training one-day course.

2. review Appendix A: Delivery Preparation Checklist, completing the checklist as a guide for their preparation.

3. continue implementing their action plans.

Thank participants for attending the workshop and for being actively involved in their learning. Encourage them to complete and implement their development plans.

Slide 4–1

Welcome to Facilitation Skills Training

Your Name
Date
Location

Slide 4–2

Presenters vs. Facilitators

- In your group:
  - Pick a recorder.
  - Brainstorm differences between "presenter" and "learning facilitator."
  - Introduce yourselves.
  - Complete the assignment in 6 minutes.
  - Present work.

Slide 4–3

How a Facilitator Differs from a Presenter

- Focus is on the learner.
- Shares control with participants.
- Credibility is from the learning environment, not expertise alone.
- Accountability for learning is shared.
- Learners are engaged on multiple levels.

Slide 4–4

Learning Objectives

- Analyze various types of learning activities

- Explain the use of the interactive lecture

- Facilitate a guided discussion

Slide 4–5

Learning Objectives

- Develop strategies to facilitate learning while handling the needs of disruptive participants

- Develop strategies to adjust on the fly in a learning event when necessary

- Prepare development plan strategies for facilitation skill practice back on the job

---

Slide 4–6

Ground Rules

- Start/stop on time
- Hold no private conversations
- Stay on topic
- Participate and share insights
- Respect others' opinions and their time to talk
- You may pass when asked to respond
- The more experienced participants coach others
- Protect confidentiality
- Turn off cell phones and pagers
- Have fun

Slide 4–7

Interactive Lecture

- In a traditional lecture:
  - Focus is on the facilitator.
  - Learners are relatively passive.
- To make the lecture interactive:
  - Ask participants questions every few minutes.
  - Invite their questions.
- Use when learners don't know very much about the content.

Slide 4–8

Guided Discussion

- *Definition:* a discussion/dialogue between facilitator and learners that is guided by a series of planned facilitator questions
- For each learning point to be brought out,
  - Craft a question.
  - Note most likely learner responses.
  - Plan follow-up comments.
- Use when learners know something about the content and can engage it.
- Use this activity to debrief other learning activities.

Slide 4–9

Structured Bridge Activity

- Learners work together.
- Uses content at a deeper level.
- Learners are more active and involved.
- Facilitator's role: organizer, monitor, and guide.
- Used with learners who have some knowledge of the content
- Provides a "bridge" between content and application.

Slide 4–10

Instructions

- In your group:
  - Read the case study, Handout 6–11.
  - Work together to answer the case questions.
  - Use Handouts 6–12, 6–13, and 6–14 as reference.
  - You have 30 minutes.
- Present recommendations for learning activities, rationales, and brief activity descriptions.

Slide 4–11

Facilitating Learning Activities Practice Setup

- Setting up instructions and monitoring learning activities
- Grouping learners in learning activities
- Sequencing learning activities and giving feedback
- Using media
- Physical presentation

Slide 4–12

Instructions

- Design and deliver a guided discussion that will teach the rest of the group about your assigned subject.
- Maximum length: 6 minutes
- After lunch
- Resources:
  - Partial handout (you add the rest!)
  - Your observations and experiences in this course so far
  - Your own experiences and intuition

Slide 4–13

Scenario

You will be facilitating a training course in a hotel. The room is a large rectangular room with a door at one end. Given a group size of 20–24, you will need only about half the room. The design of the course calls for (a) some individual work, (b) some work in pairs, and (c) some small group work.

The grouping of the participants will be changed with each group activity.

There are no breakout rooms.

Slide 4–14

Disruptive Participants

- Part 1:
  - Choose a scribe.
  - Identify and describe examples of disruptive participant behavior, and identify and discuss causal factors.
  - Present.
- Part 2:
  - Develop strategies to address disruptive behavior, using Handout 6–31.
  - Present.

Slide 4–15

Facilitator Tactics

- Not getting caught in one-on-one power struggles
- Using good-natured humor
- Connecting with the participant on a personal level
- Broadening the participation of the rest of the group
- Protecting participants as needed
- Using a separate Issues Chart or Parking Lot to postpone issues
- Recognizing the learner's point and then taking the discussion offline
- Changing the composition of small groups
- Modifying activities or instructional strategies

Slide 4–16

Instructions

- Which items are critical and which are nice to know? If you had to, would you omit any of the activities when adjusting on the fly? If so, which ones?

- How would you adjust each activity? Why?

- Take 20 minutes to make these decisions.

- Be prepared to discuss.

◆

Learning Activities

What's in This Chapter?

- ◆ Detailed instructions for using the learning activities in this program

- ◆ Tips for program facilitators

In this chapter you will find all of the learning activities included in the two-day and one-day training program agendas presented in chapters 3 and 4. In each activity description you will find the goal of the activity, time, materials, and process. The facilitator discussions in chapters 3 and 4 augment the activities as well.

The slides referred to in each of the learning activities in this chapter are numbered according to the order in which they appear in each PowerPoint presentation. You can choose individual slides to suit your customized content by opening the file you want to change, saving the file under a different name, and deleting slides you do not want to use.

Tips for Program Facilitators

This program material is unique in that it is a "train the trainer" program about training trainers (or learning facilitators, as it is expressed in the materials). Because of this uniqueness, program facilitators have two opportunities to support others' learning in the program:

1. All of the material in this program represents potential learning for you as well as for the learners in the course. There are no separate

chapters in this guide about such things as preparation, room setup, facilitating learning activities, and the like, because these are the topics in the course! If there is something that you want to brush up on before facilitating the program, seek out and review the actual course content about that topic.

2. As you facilitate these courses, you will be expected to be a role model of how to facilitate. You should use the techniques that are taught, as they are being taught, and be prepared to discuss why you did it that way—or why you decided to change it. Be prepared to use your sense of humor in discussing the (it is hoped, very few) instances when you inadvertently demonstrate how **not** to do something!

Add your personal touch as much as possible to this program by sharing stories and examples from your experiences as a learning facilitator. Also plan to use examples from your own organization to assist your participants in applying the concepts to the real world.

Prepare to be flexible and adjust on the fly in the ways suggested in the program. You can change your activities because of time constraints, learner backgrounds, goals, and needs. Knowing ahead of time how you might adjust helps you feel prepared.

Learning Activity 5–1: Presenters and Facilitators

GOALS

The goals of this activity are to

- help learners recognize the differences between presenting informa-tion and facilitating the actual learning of that information—and as a result, buy into the fact that there is much to learn about facilitation

- facilitate learner introductions.

MATERIALS

The materials needed for this activity are

- Handout 6–1: Presenter and Facilitator: What's the Difference?

- Slide 3–2: Presenters vs. Facilitators

- Slide 3–3: How a Facilitator Differs from a Presenter

- paper and pens at the learners' tables.

TIME

- 20 minutes

INSTRUCTIONS

Use slide 3–2 to give learners their instructions. They are to

- pick a recorder at their tables to take notes

- brainstorm what they believe are the differences between a presenter and a learning facilitator

- introduce themselves to each other if they don't already know each other ("Who's Here")

- take six minutes to complete the assignment.

As the facilitator:

- Give the groups a one-minute warning to "finish the point they are working on at the moment" and ask them to share their thoughts round-robin style.

  ◆ Post their thoughts on a flipchart as they share.

  ◆ Conduct the debriefing discussion: discuss their points and reinforce that they identified key information.

Distribute Handout 6–1 and show slide 3–3. Review and identify any points that were missed.

See chapter 3 for an interactive lecture debrief.

Learning Activity 5–2: Facilitator Self-Assessment

GOALS

The goals of this activity are to

- help the participants see the complexities of effective facilitation

- help the participants identify their facilitator competency development opportunities.

MATERIALS

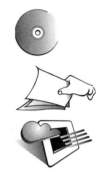

The materials needed for this activity are

- Handout 6–2: Facilitator Self-Assessment

- Slide 3–6: Areas of Facilitator Competency

- paper and pens at the learners' tables.

TIME

- 20 minutes

INSTRUCTIONS

Distribute Handout 6–2. Reveal slide 3–6 and review the categories of facilitator competencies. Ask learners if there are any competency headings or items that they don't understand, and if so, explain them.

Ask learners to take 11 minutes of "solo time" to complete the self-assessment by rating their abilities in performing the competencies. Tell them that this exercise is for development purposes only and that the more honest they are, the more beneficial the assessment will be.

When time is up, ask the participants to share their self-assessments with a partner. Allow six minutes for partners to share and discuss.

See chapter 3 for the next steps.

Learning Activity 5–3: Applying Learning Styles to Facilitation of Learning Experiences

GOAL

The goal of this activity is to

- apply concepts of learning styles to facilitating a learning experience.

MATERIALS

The materials needed for this activity are

- Handout 6–5: Learning Styles

- Handout 6–6: Recognizing Learning Styles

- Slide 3–15: Instructions

- five flipcharts and markers (one for each group).

TIME

- 25 minutes:
  - 15 minutes for identification of techniques
  - 10 minutes for presentations

INSTRUCTIONS

Show slide 3–15. Divide the group into five subgroups, assigning each group one of the learning styles (achievers, evaluators, networkers, socializers, and observers). Give each group the following instructions:

- Pick a recorder to take notes.

- Work together to identify ways or techniques to accommodate the learning needs of your assigned learning style.

- Focus on how each technique addresses the assigned learning style.

- Take 15 minutes to prepare.

- Pick a presenter to report your results to the group.

- Present your ideas to the larger group.

See chapter 3 for debriefing instructions.

Learning Activity 5–4: Structured Bridge Activities

GOALS

The goals of this activity are to

♦ help the learners identify the characteristics of a structured activity

♦ have the learners experience a structured activity.

MATERIALS

The materials needed for this activity are

♦ Slide 3–19: Instructions

♦ flipcharts and markers for each group of learners.

TIME

♦ 25 minutes:
  ♦ 15 minutes for learners' work
  ♦ 10 minutes for their presentations

INSTRUCTIONS

After briefly discussing structured activities (see chapter 3), reveal the activity instructions on slide 3–19 (keep the instructions posted throughout the activity).

♦ Pick a recorder at your table to take notes.

♦ In your group, work together to answer the following questions; make a flipchart with your responses.

  ♦ What is the biggest difference between structured activities and the activities we have examined so far?

  ♦ Why are these activities called "bridges"?

  ♦ Where do the learners get the content that they work with in a structured activity?

  ♦ What are two examples of structured activities?

- ◆ You have 15 minutes.

- ◆ Choose a presenter.

As the facilitator:

- ◆ Monitor the groups' work as the activity progresses. If a group appears stuck, ask the members a targeted question to get their thoughts on the right track.

- ◆ If they have not started making their flipcharts by approximately eight minutes in, remind them of how much time they have left.

- ◆ Give a two-minute warning.

- ◆ When time is up, have the groups present their answers round-robin style.

See chapter 3 for debriefing instructions.

Learning Activity 5–5:
Skill Practices Case Study

GOALS

The goals of this activity are to

- help learners identify the characteristics of advanced structured activities (practices), such as case studies, role plays, and demonstration and practices

- have the learners experience a skill practice case study.

MATERIALS

The materials needed for this activity are

- Handout 6–11: Facilitation Case Study

- Handout 6–12: The Case Study

- Handout 6–13: The Role Play

- Handout 6–14: The Demonstration and Practice

- Slide 3–20: Instructions

- flipcharts and markers for each group of learners.

TIME

- 60 minutes:
  - 30 minutes for learners' work
  - 15 minutes for their presentations
  - 15 minutes for debrief

INSTRUCTIONS

Form learner groups of four or five members. Pass out Handout 6–11 to all groups.

Reveal the activity instructions on slide 3–20.

Pass out Handouts 6–12, 6–13, and 6–14 to all groups.

Each group is to

- read the case study.

- work together to answer the questions in the case study.

- use Handouts 6–12, 6–13, and 6–14 as reference.

The groups have 30 minutes to work together to identify three learning activity recommendations and chart a presentation.

Participants will then present

- recommendations for learning activities

- rationales for recommendations

- brief descriptions of the actual activities.

As the facilitator:

- If the groups have not started making their flipcharts by approximately 15–20 minutes in, remind them of how much time they have left.

- Give a five-minute warning.

- When time is up, have the groups present their answers round-robin style.

See chapter 3 for debriefing instructions.

Learning Activity 5–6:
Facilitating Learning Activities Practice Setup

GOAL

The goal of this activity is to

- give learners experience and practice time in planning and facilitating a guided discussion and a structured bridge activity.

MATERIALS

The materials needed for this activity are

- Handout 6–15: Behavioral Checklist for a Structured Bridge Activity

- Handout 6–16: Behavioral Checklist for a Guided Discussion

- Handout 6–17: Setting Up Instructions and Monitoring Learning Activities (Partial)

- Handout 6–18: Grouping Learners in Learning Activities (Partial)

- Handout 6–19: Sequencing Learning Activities and Giving Feedback (Partial)

- Handout 6–20: Using Media (Partial)

- Handout 6–21: Physical Presentation Tips (Partial)

- Slide 3–21: Facilitating Learning Activities Practice Setup

- Slide 3–22: Facilitating Learning Activities

- peripheral materials such as scrap paper, markers, blank transparencies, scissors, tape, and overhead projector.

TIME

- 90–120 minutes:
  - 30 minutes to set up and give instructions
  - 60–90 minutes "lab" time

INSTRUCTIONS

Reveal slide 3–21. Explain to the learners that you are about to divide them into five groups, according to the five categories listed on the slide. Divide them into five groups. Review the activity instructions on slide 3–22. The following are the groups' assignments:

- Design and deliver a structured bridge activity with guided discussion debrief that will teach the rest of the group about your assigned subject.

- The discussion and debrief are to be a maximum of 10 minutes.

- Be prepared to deliver your discussion and debrief tomorrow (Day 2) morning.

The following are resources that the groups will use in their assignments:

- partial handout (you add the rest) (Depending on the group's assignment, Handouts 6–17 through 6–21)

- your observations and experiences in this course so far

- your own experiences and intuition.

As the facilitator:

- Distribute Handouts 6–15 and 6–16. Review the quality criteria for these two activities and tell learners that they will receive feedback in the morning according to these checklists.

- Pass out Handouts 6–17, 6–18, 6–19, 6–20, and 6–21 to groups according to their assignments. Point out to them that the handouts are "partial" and that part of their challenge is to "intuit" the remainder of the content from their experiences thus far in the class and their own backgrounds.

- Tell the learners that they will now have a "lab" during which they can design and prepare for their learning activities. Explain that you will be in the room to answer questions and make suggestions.

- Explain that they can use the various supplies in the room to augment their activities. Let them know that "artistic quality" of presentation materials won't be a factor in their activities in the morning; rather, the creative use of materials to augment and support the activities will be important.

  Note: The miscellaneous supplies enumerated in the materials list that precedes the workshop agenda (flipchart paper, water-based color markers, masking tape, sticky-notes, tent cards, colored paper, blank transparencies and markers, scissors) should be made available at this time.

◆ Tell them how long you will be available, and if applicable, how long they are permitted to stay in the meeting space to do their work. Instruct them to be prepared to begin the first activity when class begins the next morning.

◆ Stay in the room as promised and provide assistance as requested. Leave when the allotted time is up.

Learning Activity 5–7: Facilitating Learning Activities Practice

GOAL

The goal of this activity is to

- give learners experience and practice time in planning and facilitating a structured bridge activity and a debrief guided discussion.

MATERIALS

The materials needed for this activity are

- Handout 6–15: Behavioral Checklist for a Structured Bridge Activity

- Handout 6–16: Behavioral Checklist for a Guided Discussion

- Handout 6–22: Setting up Instructions and Monitoring Learning Activities (Complete)

- Handout 6–23: Grouping Learners in Learning Activities (Complete)

- Handout 6–24: Sequencing Learning Activities and Giving Feedback (Complete)

- Handout 6–25: Using Media (Complete)

- Handout 6–26: Physical Presentation Tips (Complete)

- peripheral materials such as colored paper, markers, blank transparencies, scissors, and tape.

TIME

- Three hours:
  - five presentations at 30 minutes each
  - 30 minutes to debrief activity

INSTRUCTIONS

Morning of Day 2:

Briefly review Handouts 6–15 and 6–16. Remind the groups that they have 5–10 minutes for their activities.

Begin the activities. Allow groups to choose the order they go in, or draw straws to decide the order.

For each activity (30 minutes each):

- Allow the group five minutes to set up.

- Ask them what kind of time warning they want, such as two minutes, three minutes, or more. Make a hand-lettered sign with the appropriate numeral on it and tell the learners you will hold up that time warning sign for 10–15 seconds so they can see it. Warn the learners that if they go much over the 10-minute limit, you will have to stop the activity.

- (10 minutes) The learners facilitate the activity.

- (5 minutes) When the activity is over, use the checklists to facilitate a feedback session in a format of "what went well, what could be improved?" The presenting group can comment first, then other learners. You, as the facilitator, add any last comments.

- (3 minutes) Have learners fill out the checklists with their comments and give them to the presenting group.

- (5 minutes) Distribute the complete Handouts 6–22, 6–23, 6–24, 6–25, or 6–26, for the learning activity content that applies to that presentation. Have learners review them briefly to see if any additional points should be brought out.

See chapter 3 for whole group debriefing instructions to be facilitated after all the groups have completed their activities.

Learning Activity 5–8: Room Setup

GOAL

The goal of this activity is to

- show learners how to design a room setup conducive to learning.

MATERIALS

The materials for this activity are

- Handout 6–27: Checklist for Room Setup

- Handout 6–28: Sample Room Layouts

- Slide 3–23: Scenario

- flipchart for each team

- markers.

TIME

- 40 minutes

INSTRUCTIONS

Divide the participants into four groups.

Distribute Handouts 6–27 and 6–28. Review the following scenario on slide 3–23 with the learners:

- Instruct the learners to choose a recorder at their tables to take notes, and a presenter to present their results.

- You will be facilitating a training course in a hotel. The room is a large rectangular room with a door on one end. Given a group size of 20–24, you will only need about half the room. The design of the course calls for (a) some individual work, (b) working in pairs, and (c) some small group work.

◆ Because you want to have people get to know each other and help build an appreciation for others' expertise, the grouping of the participants will be changed with each group activity.

◆ There are no breakout rooms.

Using their flipcharts and markers, the participants are to design a complete room setup to meet the program requirements while enhancing a learning environment (20 minutes).

Participants are to present their room setups with a rationale supporting their decisions (five minutes per group).

Learning Activity 5–9:
Managing Disruptive Participants

GOALS

The goals of this activity are to

- identify types of disruptive behavior

- identify the underlying causal factors contributing to disruptive behavior

- develop strategies to address disruptive behaviors.

MATERIALS

The materials needed for this activity are

- Handout 6-31: Strategies for Dealing with Disruptive Behavior

- Handout 6-32: Recognizing and Responding to Disruptive Learner Behavior

- Handout 6-33: Recommended Strategies to Deal with Disruptive Behaviors

- Slide 3–24: Disruptive Participants

- flipcharts

- markers

- masking tape.

TIME

- 15 minutes

INSTRUCTIONS

Divide the participants into four small groups. Reveal instructions on slide 3–24. Each group is to

- choose a scribe to record its responses on a flipchart and post it on the wall.

- identify and describe several types of participant behaviors that would be classified as "disruptive"

- identify and discuss the causal factors driving each disruptive behavior

- present.

After the presentations,

- distribute Handouts 6–31 and 6–32.

- conduct a debrief using instructor notes in chapter 3.

Complete this learning activity. In their groups, learners are to use Handout 6–31 and work together to develop strategies for addressing disruptive behavior (that is, fill in the spaces in the right-hand column of the handout).

Learning Activity 5–10: Adjusting on the Fly

GOAL

The goal of this activity is to

- ◆ enable learners to make preplanned "adjust on the fly" decisions.

MATERIALS

Materials needed for this activity are

- ◆ Handout 6–36: Sample Module Plan—Creating the Climate and Environment for Learning

- ◆ Slide 3–26: Instructions.

TIME

- ◆ 30 minutes

INSTRUCTIONS

Divide the participants into several groups.

Distribute Handout 6–36. Point out that this is the outline for the module that was facilitated in this course on the morning of Day 1 (yesterday).

Review the activity instructions on slide 3–26, and ask the groups to discuss the following:

- ◆ Which items are critical and which are nice to know? If you had to, would you omit any of the activities when adjusting on the fly? Which ones?

- ◆ How would you adjust each activity if you had to? Why?

The groups should take 20 minutes to work together to make these decisions, and be prepared to discuss them with the other learners.

When the groups have finished working, conduct a debriefing discussion (see chapter 3).

Learning Activity 5–11:
Structuring the Development Plan

GOAL

The goal of this activity is

- to have participants structure an action plan for their continued competency enhancement.

MATERIALS

What is needed for this activity is

- Handout 6–40: Structuring the Development Plan.

- Slide 3–27: Instructions

- Slide 3–28: Development Plans

TIME

- 20 minutes

INSTRUCTIONS

- Learners are to work on the development plan, completing as much of it as time allows.

- Learners should complete and implement the development plan on their jobs.

- Have each participant share his or her initial plans with another participant.

Learning Activity 5–12:
Presenters and Facilitators

GOALS

The goals of this activity are to

- help learners recognize the differences between presenting information and facilitating the actual learning of that information—and, as a result, buy into the fact that there is much to learn about facilitation

- facilitate learner introductions.

MATERIALS

The materials needed for this activity are

- Handout 6–1: Presenter and Facilitator: What's the Difference?

- Slide 4–2: Presenters vs. Facilitators

- Slide 4–3: How a Facilitator Differs from a Presenter

- paper and pens at the learners' tables.

TIME

- 20 minutes

INSTRUCTIONS

Use slide 4–2 to give learners their instructions. They are to

- pick a recorder at each table to take notes.

- brainstorm what they believe are the differences between a presenter and a learning facilitator.

- introduce themselves to each other if they don't already know each other ("Who's Here").

- take six minutes to complete the assignment.

As the facilitator:

- Give the groups a one-minute warning to "finish the point they are working on at the moment" and ask them to share their thoughts round-robin style.

- Post their thoughts on a flipchart as they share.

- Conduct the debriefing discussion: discuss their points and reinforce that they identified key information

Pass out Handout 6–1 and show slide 4–3. Review and identify any points that were missed.

See chapter 4 for an interactive lecture debriefing.

Learning Activity 5–13:
Skill Practices Case Study

GOALS:

The goals of this activity are to

- help learners identify the characteristics of skill practices (advanced structured activities), like case studies, role plays, and demonstration or practices

- have the learners experience a skill practice—a case study.

MATERIALS

The materials needed for this activity are

- Handout 6–11: Facilitation Case Study

- Handout 6–12: The Case Study

- Handout 6–13: The Role Play

- Handout 6–14: The Demonstration and Practice

- Slide 4–10: Instructions

- flipcharts and markers for each group of learners.

TIME

- 70 minutes:
  - 30 minutes for learner work
  - 15 minutes for their presentations
  - 15 minutes for debriefing
  - 10-minute break inserted at appropriate point

INSTRUCTIONS

Form learner groups of four to five learners. Pass out Handout 6–11, Facilitation Case Study, to all groups.

Distribute Handouts 6–12 through 6–14.

Each group is to

- read the case study.

- work together to answer the questions in the case study.

- use Handouts 6–12, 6–13, and 6–14 as reference.

The groups have 30 minutes to work together to answer the questions posed in the case study, to identify three learning activity recommendations, and chart a presentation. They will then present

- recommendations for learning activities

- rationales for recommendations

- brief descriptions of the actual activities.

As the facilitator:

- If the learners have not started making their flipcharts by approximately 15–20 minutes in, remind them of how much time they have left.

- Give a five-minute warning.

- When time is up, have the groups present their answers round-robin style.

See chapter 4 for debriefing.

Learning Activity 5–14:
Facilitating Learning Activities Practice Setup

GOAL

The goal of this activity is to

- give learners experience and practice time in planning and facilitating a guided discussion.

MATERIALS

The materials needed for this activity are

- Handout 6–16: Behavioral Checklist for a Guided Discussion

- Handout 6–17: Setting Up Instructions and Monitoring Learning Activities (Partial)

- Handout 6–18: Grouping Learners in Learning Activities (Partial)

- Handout 6–19: Sequencing Learning Activities and Giving Feedback (Partial)

- Handout 6–20: Using Media (Partial)

- Handout 6–21: Physical Presentation Tips (Partial)

- Slide 4–11: Facilitating Learning Activities Practice Setup

- Slide 4–12: Instructions

- peripheral materials such as colored paper, markers, blank transparencies, scissors, and tape.

TIME

- 70 minutes:
  - 20 minutes to set up and give instructions
  - 50 minutes for "lab"

INSTRUCTIONS

Reveal slide 4–11. Explain to the learners that you are about to divide them into five groups, according to the five categories listed on the slide. Divide them into groups. Reveal the activity instructions on slide 4–12. The following are the learners' assignments:

- Design and deliver a guided discussion that will teach the rest of the group about your assigned subject.

- Make your discussion no longer than six minutes.

- Be prepared to facilitate the guided discussion after lunch.

The following are resources that the groups will use in their assignments:

- partial handout (you add the rest) (depending on the groups' assignments, Handouts 6–17 through 6–21)

- your observations and experiences in this course so far

- your own experiences and intuition.

As the facilitator:

- Distribute Handout 6–16. Review the quality criteria for the guided discussion activity and tell learners that they will receive feedback according to this checklist.

- Pass out Handouts 6–17, 6–18, 6–19, 6–20, and 6–21 to groups according to their assignments. Point out to them that the handouts are "partial" and that part of their challenge is to "intuit" the remainder of the content from their experiences in the class thus far and their own backgrounds.

- Tell the learners that they will now have a "lab" during which they can design and prepare for their guided discussions. Explain that you will be in the room to answer questions and make suggestions.

- Explain that they have various supplies in the room that can be used to augment their activities. Let them know that "artistic quality" of presentation materials won't be a factor in their activities in the morning; rather, the creative use of materials to augment and support the activities will be important. **Note:** The miscellaneous supplies enumerated in the chapter 4 materials list (flipchart paper, water-based color markers, masking tape, sticky-notes, tent cards, colored paper, blank transparencies and markers, scissors, etc.) should be made available at this time.

- Tell them the lab is scheduled for 50 minutes, until lunch time at noon. Lunch will be from noon until 1:00, at which time the presentations will begin.

- Offer the option of shortening lunch to have more lab time.

Learning Activity 5–15: Facilitating Learning Activities Practice

GOAL

The goal of this activity is to

◆ give learners experience and practice time in planning and facilitating a guided discussion.

MATERIALS

The materials needed for this activity are

◆ Handout 6–16: Behavioral Checklist for a Guided Discussion

◆ Handout 6–22: Setting Up Instructions and Monitoring Learning Activities (Complete)

◆ Handout 6–23: Grouping Learners in Learning Activities (Complete)

◆ Handout 6–24: Sequencing Learning Activities and Giving Feedback (Complete)

◆ Handout 6–25: Using Media (Complete)

◆ Handout 6–26: Physical Presentation Tips (Complete)

◆ peripheral materials such as colored paper, markers, blank transparencies, scissors, and tape.

TIME

◆ 1 hour, 50 minutes
  ◆ Five presentations at 20 minutes each
  ◆ 10-minute break inserted as appropriate

INSTRUCTIONS

After lunch: Briefly review Handout 6–16. Remind the groups that they have six minutes for their discussion. Begin the activities. Allow groups to choose the order they go in, or draw straws to decide the order. For each activity (20 minutes per group):

◆ (5 minutes) Allow the learners a few minutes to set up.

◆ Ask them what kind of time warning they want, such as two minutes, three minutes, or more. Make a hand-lettered sign with the appropriate numeral on it and tell the learners you will hold up that time warning sign for 10–15 seconds so they can see it. Warn them that if they go much over the six-minute limit, you will have to stop the activity.

◆ (6 minutes) The learners facilitate the guided discussion.

◆ (5 minutes) When the activity is over, use the checklists to facilitate a feedback session in a format of "what went well, what could be improved:" The presenting group should comment first, then the other learners. As the facilitator, you add any last comments. Have the other learners fill out the checklists with comments and give them to the presenting group.

◆ (4 minutes) Pass out the complete handouts (6–22, 6–23, 6–24, or 6–25) for the learning activity content that applies to that specific presentation. Have learners briefly review the handouts to see if any additional points should be brought out.

See chapter 4 for instructions for final debriefing after all discussions are completed.

Learning Activity 5-16: Managing Disruptive Participants

GOALS

The goals of this activity are to

- identify types of disruptive behavior

- identify the underlying causal factors contributing to disruptive behavior

- develop strategies to address disruptive behaviors.

MATERIALS

The materials needed for this activity are

- Handout 6-31: Strategies for Dealing with Disruptive Behavior

- Handout 6-32: Recognizing and Responding to Disruptive Learner Behavior

- Handout 6-33: Recommended Strategies to Deal with Disruptive Behaviors

- Slide 3–24: Disruptive Participants

- flipcharts

- markers

- masking tape.

TIME

- 15 minutes

INSTRUCTIONS

Divide the participants into four small groups. Reveal instructions on slide 3–24. Each group is to

- choose a scribe to record its responses on a flipchart and post it on the wall.

- ◆ identify and describe several types of participant behaviors that would be classified as "disruptive"

- ◆ identify and discuss the causal factors driving each disruptive behavior

- ◆ present.

After the presentations,

- ◆ distribute Handouts 6–31 and 6–32.

- ◆ conduct a debrief using instructor notes in chapter 3.

Complete this learning activity. In their groups, learners are to use Handout 6–31 and work together to develop strategies for addressing disruptive behavior (that is, fill in the spaces in the right-hand column of the handout).

Learning Activity 5–17:
Adjusting on the Fly

GOAL

The goal of this activity is to

   ◆ enable learners to make preplanned "adjust on the fly" decisions.

MATERIALS

Materials needed for this activity are

   ◆ Handout 6–39: Sample Module Plan—Skill Practices Case Study

   ◆ Slide 4–16: Instructions.

TIME

   ◆ 30 minutes

INSTRUCTIONS

Divide the participants into several groups.

Distribute Handout 6–39. Point out that this is the outline for the module on guided discussions that was facilitated in this course earlier today

Review the activity instructions on slide 4–16, and ask the groups to address the following questions:

   ◆ Which items are critical and which are nice to know? If you had to, would you omit any of the activities when adjusting on the fly? Which ones?

   ◆ How would you adjust each activity if you had to? Why?

The groups should take 20 minutes to work together to make these decisions, and be prepared to discuss them with the other learners.

When the groups have finished working, conduct a debriefing discussion (see chapter 4).

Learning Activity 5–18:
Structuring the Development Plan

GOAL

The goal of this activity is to

- ◆ have participants structure an action plan for their continued competency development.

MATERIALS

What is needed for this activity is

- ◆ Handout 6–40: Structuring the Development Plan.

TIME

- ◆ 20 minutes

INSTRUCTIONS

Learners are to work on the development plan, completing as much of it as time allows.

Have each participant share his or her initial plans with another participant.

Learners should complete and implement the development plan on their jobs.

◆

Handouts

What's in This Chapter?

- ◆ 40 handouts for use in the one- and two-day training sessions

In this chapter you'll find all of the handouts included in the two-day and one-day training program agendas presented in chapters 3 and 4. Each handout is referred to by number in the learning activity descriptions in chapter 5 and in the agendas offered in chapters 3 and 4.

Electronic versions of the handouts are located on the CD in the file folder labeled "Handouts." For easy reference, the file naming convention follows the labels used in this book (that is, Handout 6–1, Handout 6–2, and so forth). When you select handouts for a particular workshop, you may want to rename them and sequence them with a simple numbering system that reflects the order in which your learners will use them.

Handout 6–1

Presenter and Facilitator: What's the Difference?

PRESENTER	FACILITATOR
◆ Focus is on the content	◆ Focus is on the learners
◆ Controls all—who talks, the setting, and order of content presentation	◆ Shares control with learners by getting their input and structuring the learning environment and climate accordingly
◆ Credibility is derived from subject matter expertise	◆ Credibility is derived from 　◆ creation of the learning environment 　◆ the group process 　◆ linking training to learners' jobs 　◆ flexibility to adapt to learners 　◆ support for the learner 　◆ keeping the spotlight on learners 　◆ subject matter expertise 　◆ helping learners "self-discover" content
◆ Goal is to inform the audience about the content	◆ Goal is to involve the audience in the content
◆ Possesses all of the content	◆ Shares content and "pulls" it out of the learners
◆ Addresses an audience that is mostly passive	◆ Addresses an audience that is active
◆ Is accountable for the learning	◆ Shares accountability for learning with the participants
◆ Engages learners at the thinking level	◆ Engages learners at multiple levels: cognitive, intuitive, and emotional

Handout 6–2
Facilitator Self-Assessment

Instructions: The following is a list of behaviors involved in effective facilitation skills. Given your level of experience in each of these skill areas, rate your ability to demonstrate these behaviors by placing an "x" in the appropriate box.

1 = VERY LITTLE OR NO ABILITY *(I have never done this and I know nothing about it.)*
2 = AVERAGE ABILITY *(I have done this once or twice but feel that I have a lot to learn.)*
3 = ABOVE-AVERAGE ABILITY *(I have done this several times; I understand the principles behind it and do it well.)*
4 = GREAT DEAL OF ABILITY *(I am so good at this that I could teach others.)*

SKILL AREA	1	2	3	4
Credibility				
1. I demonstrate appropriate personal and professional behavior.	☐	☐	☐	☐
2. I demonstrate subject content knowledge (depth and breadth).	☐	☐	☐	☐
3. I make linkages to organizational realities.	☐	☐	☐	☐
Learning environment and climate				
4. I involve participants in establishing and maintaining the learning environment.	☐	☐	☐	☐
5. I use opening (warm-up) activities to gain participant involvement.	☐	☐	☐	☐
6. I manage group interaction, draw in quiet participants, and manage participants who try to monopolize the interaction.	☐	☐	☐	☐
7. I integrate adult learning principles into the course delivery.	☐	☐	☐	☐
Communication skills				
8. I use appropriate verbal and nonverbal communication methodology.	☐	☐	☐	☐
9. I use examples that are familiar to participants.	☐	☐	☐	☐
10. I provide complete and timely feedback to participants.	☐	☐	☐	☐
11. I provide time for participants to structure/frame and ask questions and voice concerns or issues.	☐	☐	☐	☐
Presentation/Facilitation skills				
12. I effectively use my voice (tone, projection, inflection), gestures, and eye contact.	☐	☐	☐	☐
13. I effectively use examples, such as stories and personal experiences, as well as humor.	☐	☐	☐	☐
14. I effectively use various questioning techniques.				
15. I effectively paraphrase or restate participants' questions, comments, and observations in an effort to make sure I (and the other learners) understand.	☐	☐	☐	☐
16. I promote participant discussion and involvement.	☐	☐	☐	☐
17. I keep discussions on topic and activities focused on outcomes.	☐	☐	☐	☐

continued on next page

Handout 6–2, continued
Facilitator Self-Assessment

SKILL AREA	1	2	3	4

Instructional/Learning strategies

18. I implement a variety of instructional or learning strategies (such as guided discussions, case studies, role play, small group work with feedback, and assessments). ☐ ☐ ☐ ☐

19. I plan and facilitate debriefs so that all learning is processed. ☐ ☐ ☐ ☐

20. I adjust activities, time, pace, content, and sequencing to accommodate specific learners' needs. ☐ ☐ ☐ ☐

Media

21. I effectively use media (video, overheads, computer projection, wallboards, props, and flipcharts) as needed. ☐ ☐ ☐ ☐

22. I demonstrate an ability to substitute, change, or add media as needed. ☐ ☐ ☐ ☐

Source: ©2003 Performance Advantage Group; adapted with permission from Performance Advantage Group.

Handout 6–3

Factors for Room Setup

The following are factors to be considered when determining the best layout for your room setup:

- ◆ The number of participants
- ◆ The types of learning activities
- ◆ The number of teams
- ◆ The number of members on each team
- ◆ Physical limitations of the room, such as size and configuration
- ◆ Required equipment for the facilitator and teams
- ◆ The facilitator's personal space
- ◆ Facilitation delivery style—podium, lectern, or open-style
- ◆ Temperature of the room, gauged in accordance with how many people will be there
- ◆ Peripheral materials and methods
- ◆ Refreshments

Handout 6–4

Aligning Learning Activities and Media with Learning Preferences

KINESTHETIC LEARNING PREFERENCE ACTIVITIES AND MEDIA	AUDITORY LEARNING PREFERENCE ACTIVITIES AND MEDIA	VISUAL LEARNING PREFERENCE ACTIVITIES AND MEDIA
Supervised practice on the job	Lectures	Reading
Simulations	Discussions	Diagramming
Paper-and-pencil tests	Demonstrations	Creating charts and graphs
Physical analogies	Brainstorming	Observing demonstrations
Note taking	Question-and-answer sessions	Training manuals
Flowcharting	Coaching	Handouts
Group projects	Panel discussions	Flowcharts
Role playing	Group or individual presentations	Flipcharts
Physical demonstrations	Group projects	Wallboards and posters
Hands-on activities	Small group work	Whiteboards
Building things	Rhymes	Reference materials
Writing on flipcharts or wallcharts	Acronyms	Lists of parts or definitions
Puzzles	Mnemonics	Films
Charades	Metaphors	Maps
Whiteboards	Definitions	Color and graphics
Tools	Music; songs and lyrics	Art works
Props	Films	Slides, photos, and PowerPoint presentations
Toys	Audiovisuals	Interactive computer simulations
Job aids	"War stories"	
Interactive computer simulations	Interactive computer simulations	

Handout 6–5
Learning Styles

Achievers

- focus on doing and accomplishing results, and are good at finding practical uses for ideas and theories.
- enjoy being involved in new and challenging experiences as well as carrying out plans to meet those challenges.
- have the ability to solve problems, make decisions, and develop action plans based on implementing solutions to questions or problems.
- like to accept the lead role in addressing those challenges.
- like sequence and logical order and clear, step-by-step directions.
- are not strongly oriented toward people.
- have a tendency to take control with little regard for others' feelings.

Evaluators

- like to analyze a situation.
- use a logical process to resolve issues.
- ask many detailed questions and, in so doing, collect a great deal of information.
- are very concerned about working within the existing guidelines.
- are good at assimilating a wide range of information and putting it into concise, logical form, such as lists, charts, or planning tools.
- are more interested in the basis and application of theory, and less interested in building relationships.
- are concerned that theory presented is logically sound, exact, and supported by facts.

Networkers

- like to develop close relationships with others and to avoid interpersonal conflict.
- have good listening skills that enable them to develop strong people networks.
- are more compliant than others, and thus are easily swayed; they try to avoid risks and seek consensus.
- are slower than others to make decisions.
- seldom disagree with others' opinions; rather, are supportive of others and welcome collaboration.
- take time to build trust and get personally acquainted with others.
- need direct feedback as a means of support.

Socializers

- like to talk and share ideas or stories.
- enjoy the spotlight and are fun-loving.
- like to get multiple perspectives.
- are good at selling their ideas to others and building alliances.

continued on next page

Handout 6–5, continued
Learning Styles

- are not concerned with details or facts.
- like to keep a fast pace and make quick, spontaneous decisions.
- provide humor.
- will volunteer to make the presentation when working in a group.

Observers

- like to view concrete situations from many different vantage points of view.
- prefer to observe and conceptualize rather than take action.
- are reflective thinkers.
- enjoy situations that call for generating not just many ideas, but also a wide range of ideas.
- are more interested in abstract ideas and concepts, and less interested in building relationships.
- want to take time to reflect and conceptualize.
- don't like to "wing it."

Handout 6–6
Recognizing Learning Styles

ROLE	VERBAL CUE	LEARNER BEHAVIOR
Achiever	◆ Tells, does little asking ◆ Is blunt and to-the-point ◆ Asks for clear directions ◆ Asks for clear, concise answers ◆ Asks for application to the job	◆ Talks a lot ◆ Takes charge, likes to be the leader ◆ Follows the participant guide, page by page and doesn't like to deviate ◆ Demonstrates little patience for non-task-related activities
Evaluator	◆ Asks for data, facts, and sources ◆ Makes focused comments on the topic ◆ Offers little personal sharing ◆ Wants the details	◆ Is task oriented ◆ Follows directions ◆ Challenges others' expertise ◆ Develops steps to accomplish activities
Networker	◆ Asks many questions ◆ Does little telling ◆ Vocalizes support for others' opinions ◆ Seeks attention and feedback	◆ Engages in effective listening ◆ Seeks collaboration and consensus ◆ Reserves personal opinions ◆ Avoids conflict ◆ Develops close relationships ◆ Builds trust
Socializer	◆ Shares experiences ◆ Tells stories ◆ Digresses and gets off the subject ◆ Readily expresses personal opinions ◆ Talks a lot ◆ Uses persuasive language	◆ Makes quick, spontaneous decisions without all the information ◆ Gets multiple perspectives ◆ Has fun ◆ Likes group activities ◆ Likes discussions
Observer	◆ Likes to conceptualize, and appreciates "what if?" discussions ◆ Asks questions or makes comments off the direct subject ◆ Makes "what about this?" statements ◆ Makes future application to discussions	◆ Provides several alternatives to a problem or situation ◆ Easily gets off the subject ◆ Wants fuller discussion on the idea ◆ Is not concerned with concrete application of the ideas

Handout 6–7

Aligning Learning Activities with Learning Preferences and Styles

LEARNING ACTIVITY	VISUAL PREFERENCE	AUDITORY PREFERENCE	KINESTHETIC PREFERENCE	ACHIEVER STYLE	EVALUATOR STYLE	NETWORKER STYLE	SOCIALIZER STYLE	OBSERVER STYLE
Lecture		X		X	X			
Handouts	X			X	X			X
Group discussion		X				X	X	X
Role play			X	X	X		X	X[1]
Group work at a flipchart	X	X	X			X	X	X
Case study		X		X	X			X
Hands-on practice			X	X				
Note taking	X		X		X			X
Games	X	X	X	X		X	X	
Small group work		X		X[2]		X	X	X[3]
Activity debriefing		X		X	X			X
Action planning			X	X	X			X
Brainstorming	X	X	X	X		X	X	X

Notes:

1. If they observe and don't participate in the action.
2. If they have a leadership role.
3. If opportunity is given to comment on observations during the activity.

Source: Adapted with permission from Deborah Davis Tobey and Deb Tobey LLC, 2004.

Handout 6–8
The Interactive Lecture

Definition

A lecture in which the focus is more on the facilitator than on the learners, and in which learners are relatively passive. The challenge is to get as much learner engagement as possible.

Purpose

To disseminate information, increase awareness, and help participants understand concepts

How to proceed

1. The facilitator presents content (a mini-lecture lasting only a few minutes).

2. The facilitator then invites participation by questioning the learners and by inviting their questions.

3. The facilitator continues to share content and invite participation throughout the entire activity. By inviting participation, what is normally thought of as a lecture *by* the facilitator becomes a discussion *with* the learners.

Appropriate to use when . . .

Learners know relatively little about the content, and therefore must learn about it before they can interact with it.

Tips

◆ Identify questions that will invite learner engagement, and plan intervals when you might ask the questions. Even learners having little or no experience with the subject can answer a question from their own experiences.

◆ Plan the intervals at which you might ask the participants if they have questions.

◆ Never deliver a "straight lecture" for more than 10–15 minutes without inviting participation in some way.

◆ Other activities during which it's important to creating interaction by asking questions include reading books, handouts; watching videos/films; using slides, overhead transparencies, PowerPoint presentations; pre-work; note taking; and completing self-assessments, such as quizzes and checklists.

Handout 6–9

The Guided Discussion

Definition

A discussion or dialogue between the facilitator and the learners in which the facilitator asks specific, planned questions designed to draw learning points from the learners.

Purpose

To disseminate information, increase awareness, and help participants understand concepts.

How to proceed

1. Identify the learning points to be brought out in the discussion.

2. For each learning point, the facilitator should

   ◆ craft a question

   ◆ note the most likely learner responses

   ◆ plan follow-up comments to augment learners' comments, and go on to the next question.

Appropriate to use when . . .

Learners already know something about the content, and can readily engage with it at some level.

Tips

◆ Use a guided discussion to "debrief" learning activities, after a structured exercise or skill practice is complete. It's designed to close the gaps in the learning, summarize the main points, and help the learners apply the content to the job.

◆ In a debrief, ask open-ended questions, such as

   ◆ What happened in the activity?

   ◆ How did that make you feel?

   ◆ What principles or generalizations can you infer from it?

   ◆ How will you apply it going forward?

   ◆ What went well?

   ◆ What could have been done better?

   ◆ How does this apply to your job?

   ◆ What will you do differently in the future?

◆ Make sure that your augmenting comments for each question add more content to the discussion; they should not simply repeat what the participants have said.

Handout 6–10
The Structured Bridge Activity

Definition

A structured activity is an activity in which the learners participate, usually working together. It is structured, though not led, by the facilitator. Structured activities are the "bridge" of discovery between knowledge and skills.

Purpose

To help learners engage with content at a deeper level by thinking through a concept, inferring from it to generate principles, and applying it to different situations or to "discover" the content that they already know.

How to proceed

1. Form learner groups.

2. Post instructions for their work together. The instructions will explain

   ◆ what they will do (answer a set of questions, build an object, discuss a subject, and the like)

   ◆ what result they will produce, such as a presentation, a report, or a model

   ◆ how much time they have to complete the assignment.

3. Start the activity.

4. Monitor the learners' progress; walk around the room and answer any questions.

5. Give a time warning.

6. When time is up, ask groups to produce or present their results.

7. Conduct a debriefing discussion.

Appropriate to use when . . .

The learners know enough about the content to accomplish the task. They have learned the content in a previous learning activity, or they already knew it before they began the course. The activity is facilitated first, before the content is revealed, so the learners have "first crack" at discovering the content for themselves. After all the groups have reported, present the content in a debriefing format to ensure that all the points have been made.

Tips

◆ Structured activities can encompass a variety of activities, not just a small group discussion. Some examples of structured activities, in order of increasing learner involvement, include

   ◆ *solo work:* learners are given an assignment to work on alone (such as fill out a questionnaire or analyze a problem), then discuss it with others.

continued on next page

Handout 6–10, continued
The Structured Bridge Activity

- *small group discussion:* small groups of learners are given a topic to discuss or questions to answer; they work together, and then present their results.

- *group inquiry:* learners are provided with content, and they work together to identify questions they have about the content.

- *information search:* learners are given reference materials and must search through them for answers to questions presented by the facilitator. In a blended learning experience (in which face-to-face learning and e-learning are combined), the "search" may involve using the Internet to conduct inquiries or to download information.

- *small group assignment/problem-solving:* small groups of learners are given a problem to solve, a situation to analyze, a list of principles or guidelines to develop in response to a problem, and so on.

- *peer teaching:* small groups of learners study the material, then teach it to the other participants or groups within the class. Determining the teaching methodology is part of the activity, and is left up to the groups.

- *games (for example, "Jeopardy," "Bingo," "Concentration"):* a version of a popular game can be developed to assist learners in remembering, comprehending, and applying content that has been presented.

Handout 6–11
Facilitation Case Study

John Fiat, the new training facilitator at the Ace Driving School, was preparing to facilitate his first course, called "Driving Skills for Novices." He sighed in frustration. He'd just spent several hours poring over his Leader's Guide, and felt as if he had driven right into a brick wall. The course content was clear—but the learning activities were not.

John decided to take a break and walked into the coffee room. Just pouring her coffee was Sara Porsche, another of the Ace facilitators. Sara took one look at John's face, and said, "Uh-oh—I see trouble! What's going on, John?"

John allowed himself one more sigh, and said, "Sara, I'm having the hardest time trying to figure out how to facilitate the learning activities in this 'Novice' course. The content's great, but the Leader's Guide is very sparse on instructions for facilitation."

Sara smiled sympathetically. "Maybe I can help. Give me an example."

John responded, "Well, in the section on rules of the road, there's a segment on road etiquette. The content is pretty straightforward—I'm supposed to conduct a guided discussion on the six most common driving etiquette situations and how to decide what to do in each. Then the Leader's Guide says, 'Conduct a case study in which learners decide what to do in each of the situations presented on the handout.' How do I facilitate a case study on this?"

Sara said, "Hmmm. So the skill involved here is being able to make a decision on the spot according to the rules of road etiquette. What else are you struggling with?"

John answered, "OK, here's another one. In the section on interpersonal driving skills, there's a segment on how to resolve conflict after a fender-bender. The activity on the content is right there—'Give an interactive lecture on the five steps to an effective conflict resolution.' But after that, the Guide simply says, 'Conduct a role play activity in which the learners practice this skill.' What do I do?"

Sara asked, "So the learners are supposed to role-play specific steps in a conversation?" When John nodded, she said, "I've got some ideas, but tell me if you're facing any other issues."

John exclaimed, "All right! Ideas are what I need. Here's the last one that has me stymied: There's a driving practice section in the course in which they're to learn various methods of driving in different situations. For example, there's a section on how to drive in foggy conditions. I've got visuals and diagrams and all of that to show them how to do it, but then the Leader's Guide says, 'Conduct a demonstration and practice session on driving in foggy conditions.' How am I supposed to do that in a classroom?"

Sara responded, "John, I don't think these examples are as hard as they might look at first glance. Let's set some time for later on today and I can share some ideas with you."

continued on next page

Handout 6–11, continued
Facilitation Case Study

Questions Regarding the Case Study on Etiquette:

- ◆ How would John set this up? What skill is addressed? What materials would he use?
- ◆ What would he have the learners do as part of the case study activity?
- ◆ What potential pitfalls should he watch for as he facilitates the activity?
- ◆ How will he measure the learners' success in solving the case?

Questions Regarding the Role Play on Resolving a Conflict Situation:

- ◆ How would John set this up? What skill is addressed? What materials would he use?
- ◆ What types of role play should he consider?
- ◆ What factors will be important for him to consider?
- ◆ How will he measure the learners' success in enacting the role play?

Questions Regarding the Demonstration and Practice Session on Driving in Foggy Conditions:

- ◆ How would John set this up? What skill is addressed? What materials would he use?
- ◆ What would he have the learners do as part of the practice?
- ◆ How will he measure the learners' success in the practice segment?

Handout 6–12
The Case Study

Definition

A skill practice (complex structured activity) in which learners work together to solve a situation/problem.

Purpose

To help learners practice a "mental" skill, that is, something that learners "do with" concepts.

How to proceed

1. Form learner groups.

2. Hand out the case study problem situation.

3. Post instructions for their work together. The instructions will explain

   ◆ what they will do (work together to investigate and resolve the problems or issues presented in the case)

   ◆ what result(s) they will produce, such as a solution or recommendations

   ◆ how much time they have to complete the assignment.

4. Start the activity.

5. Monitor their progress; walk around the room and answer any group's questions.

6. Give a time warning.

7. When time is up, ask the groups to produce or present their results. They may do so verbally or accompanied with a visual, such as a flipchart presentation.

8. Conduct a debriefing discussion.

Appropriate to use when . . .

The learners are ready to practice a "mental" skill, such as synthesizing information, analyzing a situation, evaluating something or someone (for instance, a potential vendor).

Tips

◆ Mix more-experienced learners with less-experienced learners to work on a case study.

◆ Mental tasks are product oriented—that is, a learner-produced outcome must meet certain criteria. These tasks or skills usually have more than one right answer.

◆ Measure learners' success at this activity by developing a list of "quality criteria" (what a good answer would "look like"), and assessing their activity outcome according to those criteria.

Handout 6–13
The Role Play

Definition

A skill practice (complex structured activity) in which learners enact various roles or activities to solve a problem, produce a result, or develop an interpersonal skill.

Purpose

To help learners practice an "interpersonal" skill, as in something that learners "do with" people.

How to proceed

1. Form learner groups according to the role-play setup (see below for descriptions of various types of setups).

2. Hand out the role descriptions.

3. Post instructions for their work together. The instructions will explain

   ◆ what they will do (enact the role play within the setup of the activity)

   ◆ what result(s) they will produce as a result of their interpersonal exchange in the role play, such as a solution or recommendations

   ◆ how much time they have to complete the assignment.

4. Start the activity.

5. Monitor their progress:

   ◆ if they're working together in groups to produce their role play, monitor by walking around and answering questions

   ◆ if role play is to be enacted in front of the whole class, provide directions, and start and stop the actors as needed.

6. When role play is over, conduct a debriefing discussion.

Appropriate to use when . . .

The learners are ready to practice an "interpersonal" skill, such as communicating information, persuading or influencing, and giving feedback.

Tips

◆ There are many role-play setups that can be chosen by the instructional designer of the course you facilitate. In ascending order of difficulty and challenge for the learners, they are

   ◆ videotaped (or instructor-enacted) role play that learners watch; they critique the outcome.

   ◆ scripted role play, in which two learners interact in front of the group by simply reading from a script.

continued on next page

Handout 6–13, continued

The Role Play

- ◆ instructor-led role play (*option a*), in which the instructor plays the role to be critiqued by the learners; the other players are given a situation description or script and act within that description.

- ◆ instructor-led role play (*option b*), in which a volunteer learner plays the role to be critiqued, and interacts with the instructor.

- ◆ small group role play, in which participants trade off roles with each other in round-robin style, and use course materials to critique one another; the players are given a situation description and act within that description.

- ◆ fishbowl, in which one role play at a time is enacted; volunteer learners enact the role play in front of the whole group and then are critiqued.

- ◆ free-form or improvised role play, in which a very general scenario is given to the participants and they "go with the flow" to enact the outcome.

- ◆ Interpersonal tasks can be either product oriented or process oriented:

  - ◆ In a product-oriented role play, the outcome produced by the enactors must meet certain quality criteria. The assumption is that if the enactors' behaviors meet the criteria, then the appropriate situation outcome will be reached. Measure learners' success at this activity by developing a list of "quality criteria" (what a good answer would "look like") and assessing their activity outcome according to the criteria.

  - ◆ In a process-oriented role play, the players must follow specific interpersonal steps to produce the desired outcome. The assumption is that if learners follow the required steps, the desired situation outcome will occur. Measure learners' success at this activity by developing a list of "interpersonal steps" and having an observer check off each step as it's demonstrated. This version of role play is sometimes called *behavior modeling.*

Handout 6–14
The Demonstration and Practice

Definition

A skill practice (complex structured activity) in which learners watch a demonstration of a skill, and then practice that skill with feedback from the facilitator.

Purpose

To help learners practice a "physical" skill, as in something that learners "do with" things.

How to proceed

1. Develop a "behavioral checklist" tool that contains the steps of the physical process being learned (that is, the steps in typing, or steps in a cockpit run-through, and the like) prior to facilitating the demonstration and practice.

2. Set up the physical demonstration in front of the learners. This setup must be the real thing (for example, if they're learning to type on a keyboard, there should be an actual keyboard) or the most close-as-possible simulation of the real thing (such as cockpit simulator demonstrations for aspiring pilots who can't be in a real cockpit while learning).

3. Distribute the demonstration behavioral checklist.

4. Demonstrate the physical skill while verbally "walking" the learners through the items on the checklist.

5. Have each person practice the skill while being observed by the facilitator or a fellow participant using the checklist.

6. Give feedback according to how well each learner adhered to the checklist.

Appropriate to use when . . .

The learners are ready to practice a physical skill, such as operating a piece of equipment, lifting an object that requires a special technique, installing a piece of software, or using technological equipment to support a presentation.

Tip

◆ Physical tasks are process oriented—that is, learners must follow specific physical steps to produce the desired outcome. The assumption is that if learners follow the required steps, the desired outcome or product will result.

Handout 6–15
Behavioral Checklist for a Structured Bridge Activity

Instructions for the observer: As you observe the structured bridge activity, mark "yes" or "no" for each of the items on this checklist. In the space reserved for comments, make points you'll want to make during the feedback session.

Group: _____

Topic: _____

QUESTION	YES	NO
1. Were the learners grouped appropriately? Comments:	☐	☐
2. Were the activity instructions clear? Comments:	☐	☐
3. Were the activity instructions visible throughout the activity? Comments:	☐	☐
4. Were the learners involved? Comments:	☐	☐
5. Did the facilitator(s) monitor the activity by walking around and being available for questions? Comments:	☐	☐
6. Was a time warning given to the learners? Comments:	☐	☐

Handout 6–16
Behavioral Checklist for a Guided Discussion

Instructions for the observer: As you observe the guided discussion debrief activity, mark "yes" or "no" for each of the items on this checklist. In the comments space, note the points you'll want to make during the feedback session.

Group: _____

Topic: _____

QUESTION	YES	NO
1. Did the facilitator(s) use a series of questions to guide the learners into discovery of the learning points? *Comments:*	☐	☐
2. Did the facilitator(s) pause so the learners had the opportunity to answer each question? *Comments:*	☐	☐
3. Were the learners engaged to the point where they responded to the questions? *Comments:*	☐	☐
4. Did the facilitator(s) follow up the learners' responses with more content to augment their answers? *Comments:*	☐	☐
5. Did the facilitator(s) transition to a new question and learning point after making the augmenting remarks? *Comments:*	☐	☐

6. What other comments or suggestions do you have?

Handout 6–17

Setting Up Instructions and Monitoring Learning Activities (Partial)

Instructions for the learners:

◆ Directions must be explicit. Make sure they include what the learners are to do, in what order, step-by-step, for how long, using what materials, and so forth.

◆ Keep the instructions visible because _____.

◆ Explain the purpose of the activity because _____.

◆ Use a reader-friendly format. Include bullets, heads, and subheads as necessary to make the instructions as easy to understand as possible.

◆ Some learners will literally "freeze" if _____.

◆ Some learners become embarrassed if _____.

Monitoring Activities:

Here are typical items that you will attend to while monitoring:

◆ Reiterating or re-explaining the _____.

◆ Providing assistance if learners are stuck. If you discover that a group of learners is truly stumped about how to accomplish the task you have assigned, you might

_____.

◆ Assessing whether learners need more or less time to complete the task. If they

appear to be working hard, and the original time limit is up, _____.

If they obviously are finished and are sidetracking into conversations, _____

_____.

◆ Listening in on discussions. You want to find out _____.

◆ Providing "time warnings" when learners' time is almost up, so _____.

Handout 6–18
Grouping Learners in Learning Activities (Partial)

Key principle

Form groups of different sizes at different times because _____.

Group sizes

Individuals, pairs, trios, small groups, large groups, or the entire class

Factors that affect the facilitator's grouping decisions

◆ *Shyness of participants:* _____.

◆ *Controversial nature of the content:* _____.

◆ *What the learners will actually do in the activity:* The complexity of the task, how much the learners will move around, and how they will interact with each other (talking, building something, writing, and such). Generally speaking, the more complex the task (numerous steps, a lot of movement, or higher difficulty), the

_____ the group should be.

◆ *Progression in the training course:* Usually, the earlier in the course, the _____

the groups should be because _____.

◆ *The experience, knowledge, and skills of the participants:* _____.

Grouping methods

◆ *Random grouping:* To group learners randomly, simply have them count off by the

number of groups you need (for instance, count 1, 2, 3, 4 if you need _____ groups).

◆ *Learner-choice grouping:* This method gives the learners a choice and allows them to join a group according to their interests in the subject. This method will work if

_____.

◆ *Experience-level grouping:* Have the learners mix according to experience so that each group has at least one member experienced in the subject matter who can act as an informal coach. This is beneficial to experienced learners as well as novice learners

because _____ and _____.

continued on next page

Handout 6–18, continued
Grouping Learners in Learning Activities (Partial)

♦ *Assessment tool grouping:* If you're using an individual assessment tool, such as leadership style, there might be a time when you want learners who have similar outcomes to work together (for example, you would put all the learners of one

leadership style together in each group). If you do that, be prepared to _____

_____. Don't group learners according to

assessment tool outcomes if what has been assessed is skills or knowledge, because

_____.

♦ *Seating arrangement grouping:* In some cases, you have a setup that restricts movement of participants, and the setup dictates how grouping will work. A classic example is the pit style, fixed-table-and-chairs arrangement. In a situation such as this, you can group participants by having them swivel their chairs to work with those behind them.

♦ *Organization/function grouping:* Group learners from the same organization or functional area within an organization. This can enhance application to the job. Alternatively, if the course content is sensitive, consider not having them in the same group.

♦ *Organizational level grouping:* Mix the learners so that you have management, professional, and administrative people in a group. Alternatively, you may want to have homogeneous groups to deal with specific company issues.

Handout 6–19
Sequencing Learning Activities and Giving Feedback (Partial)

Sequence

The sequence of learning activities should vary in pace, intensity, and level of learner involvement. This is useful not only in meeting the needs of varied learning styles, but also

in helping the learners _____.

For example, it would not be advisable to have the following lesson sequence:

1. role play

2. structured exercise

3. application activity

4. debriefing discussion.

You, and they, would be exhausted! A better example of sequence is

1. _____

2. _____

3. _____

4. _____

5. _____.

Adding in _____ provides rest stops between more intense activities.

Sequencing Tips

◆ Build the learners' interest with easy content first, and then introduce more demanding content.

◆ Sequence activities so that _____
before putting them together in a comprehensive skill practice.

◆ Always have a debriefing discussion when an activity is over because _____

_____.

Providing Feedback to Learners

◆ A key ingredient in sequencing is in deciding when and how to provide feedback to the learners.

continued on next page

Handout 6–19, continued

Sequencing Learning Activities and Giving Feedback (Partial)

◆ When a learner responds during a discussion, you want to affirm her or him and, if you can, affirm the given response. You may say things such as _____

_____.

◆ In other cases, the respondent may provide a superficial answer, and you want more

depth. In such a case, make comments like _____

_____.

Although you're affirming, you're also letting the learner know that there is more learning to be gained from the question.

◆ A more difficult situation occurs when the learner's response is not correct. This is

where you can't afford to agree, because _____.

In such a case, you can say something along the lines of _____

_____.

◆ Don't accept answers that are superficial, incomplete, or wrong. Your role is to help the participants learn.

◆ Tests and assessments also are ways to provide immediate feedback. These can be written or oral. Because they're used for development, it's important that you

_____.

◆ Debriefings provide great opportunities to give feedback to learners, both during learning activities and, especially, after an activity is complete, because

_____.

Handout 6–20
Using Media (Partial)

Flipcharts and Easels

When to use

◆ At informal learning events

◆ _____

Tips

◆ Make your writing legible and large (six lines per page, letters two inches high).

◆ _____

◆ _____

◆ _____

Pluses and minuses

+ _____

− _____

Overhead Transparencies

When to use

◆ Blank transparencies can be used to generate material and items on the spot.

◆ _____

Tips

◆ Talk to the learners, not to the glass in front of you or the screen behind you.

◆ _____

◆ _____

◆ _____

Pluses and minuses

+ _____

− _____

Whiteboards

When to use

◆ At informal learning events

◆ _____

continued on next page

Handout 6–20, continued

Using Media (Partial)

Tips

- ◆ _____
- ◆ _____
- ◆ _____

Pluses and minuses

- + _____
- + _____
- − _____

PowerPoint Slides, Digital Presentations, or Photographic Slides

When to use

- ◆ At formal learning events
- ◆ _____

Tips

- ◆ Use large, sans serif fonts.
- ◆ _____
- ◆ _____
- ◆ _____

Pluses and minuses

- + _____
- − _____

Videos and DVDs

When to use

- ◆ Good for behavioral modeling (watch someone doing right or wrong)
- ◆ _____

Tips

- ◆ Make sure there are enough monitors for all to see
- ◆ _____
- ◆ _____

continued on next page

Handout 6–20, continued

Using Media (Partial)

Pluses and minuses

+ _____

− _____

Written Materials

When to use

◆ You want learners to have references and takeaways

◆ _____

Tips

◆ Use colors and graphics

◆ _____

◆ _____

◆ _____

Pluses and minuses

+ _____

− _____

Props and Objects

When to use

◆ You want to make a point especially memorable

Tips

◆ Use your imagination.

◆ _____

◆ _____

◆ _____

Pluses and minuses

+ _____

− _____

Source: Adapted with permission from Deborah Davis Tobey and Deb Tobey LLC, 2003.

Handout 6–21
Physical Presentation Tips (Partial)

Voice

◆ Enunciate and speak clearly.

◆ _____

◆ _____

Nonverbal behaviors

◆ Eye contact: _____

◆ _____

◆ _____

Body language

◆ Gestures: _____

◆ _____

◆ _____

Posture

◆ Feet flat on the floor

◆ _____

◆ _____

Dress and appearance

◆ Clean

◆ _____

◆ _____

Handout 6–22

Setting Up Instructions and Monitoring Learning Activities (Complete)

Instructions for the learners:

- ◆ Directions must be explicit. Make sure they include what the learners are to do, in what order, step-by-step, for how long, using what materials, and so forth.

- ◆ Keep the instructions visible. Although you might present the instructions verbally at the start, the instructions also must be visible at all times during the activity on a flipchart, slide, or handout. You don't want your activity to be derailed by the learners constantly asking, "Now what is it we're supposed to do?"

- ◆ Explain the purpose—tell the learners why they're going to participate in the activity. Some learners are unwilling to participate unless they know how the activity will be useful.

- ◆ Use a reader-friendly format. Include bullets, heads, and subheads as necessary to make the instructions as easy to understand as possible.

  - ◆ Some learners literally will "freeze" if they don't have instructions; they can't function unless they know where they're going and what they're doing.

  - ◆ Some learners become embarrassed if they don't do the activity "right," even if it's because the instructions weren't clear.

Monitoring Activities:

When the learners work on their own, you must remain in the room, be available for questions and coaching, and "wander" to make sure the groups are working effectively. Some typical items that you will attend to while monitoring include the following:

- ◆ *Reiterating or re-explaining the activity instructions:* Although keeping instructions visible helps in this area, inevitably some learners will ask, "Now what are we supposed to do?"

- ◆ *Providing assistance if learners are stuck:* If you discover that a group of learners is truly stumped about how to accomplish the task you've assigned, you may stop beside the group and assist members by asking targeted questions to get them on the right track. Very rarely should you just tell them—but subtle assistance is appropriate at times.

- ◆ *Assessing whether they need more or less time to complete the task:* If they appear to be working hard, and the original time limit is up, you can announce that they have extra time. If they're obviously finished and are sidetracking into conversations, say, "I can see that everyone is finished; let's come back together and see what you came up with." If one group finishes early and is sidetracking, you can add an additional task, taking those learners into more depth or addressing the application to the job.

- ◆ *Listening in on discussions:* You want to find out the learners' "hot topics" in their work together; hear what ideas they have, and pick up on their issues and concerns. When you conduct the debriefing discussion, you'll be able to "speak their language."

- ◆ *Providing "time warnings"* when their time is almost up, so they can finish their discussions and not feel interrupted.

Handout 6–23
Grouping Learners in Learning Activities (Complete)

Key principle

Form groups of different sizes at different times to adjust to the type of activity and for variety's sake.

Group sizes

Individuals, pairs, trios, small groups, large groups, or the entire class

Factors that affect the facilitator's grouping decisions

♦ *Shyness of participants:* Participants who are more reserved will open up more in smaller groups.

♦ *Controversial nature of the content:* The more challenging, controversial, or uncomfortable the material, the smaller the groups should be. People are less likely to open up about uncomfortable subjects in larger groups.

♦ *What the learners will actually do in the activity:* The complexity of the task, how much the learners will move around, and how they will interact with each other (talking, building something, writing, and such). Generally speaking, the more complex the task (numerous steps, a lot of movement, or higher difficulty), the smaller the group.

♦ *Progression in the training course:* Usually, the earlier in the course, the smaller the groups should be. When the learners don't know each other, it's less threatening to interact in a pair or trio. Later on, when the learners are better acquainted, they are more comfortable speaking and participating in larger groups.

♦ *The experience, knowledge, and skills of the participants:* The deeper the learners' backgrounds with the content, the smaller the groups can be. When the learners don't know very much about the content, groups must be larger so there is more discussion, sharing, and synergy as they strive to "discover" new content.

Grouping methods

♦ *Random grouping:* To group learners randomly, simply have them count off by the number of groups you need (for instance, count 1, 2, 3, 4 if you need to have four groups).

♦ *Learner-choice grouping:* This method gives the learners a choice and allows them to join a group according to their interests in the subject. As long as your groups come out fairly even in number, the activity will work.

♦ *Experience-level grouping:* Have the learners mix according to experience so that each group has at least one member experienced in the subject matter who can act as an informal coach. This method spreads out the experience so less experienced learners can be with someone who has "been there, done that." It's also a good

continued on next page

Handout 6–23, continued

Grouping Learners in Learning Activities (Complete)

technique for engaging experienced learners at a time when the material may be a little too easy for them.

◆ *Assessment tool grouping:* If you're using an individual assessment tool, such as leadership style, there might be a time when you want learners who have similar outcomes to work together (for example, you would put all the learners of one leadership style together in each group). If you do that, be prepared to join and help a group that happens to have significantly fewer members than the other groups. Don't group learners according to assessment tool outcomes if what has been assessed is skills or knowledge because putting learners together who are at the same skill or knowledge level does not benefit their learning, and it has a tendency to stigmatize.

◆ *Seating arrangement grouping:* In some cases, you have a setup that restricts movement of participants, and the setup dictates how grouping will work. A classic example is the pit style, fixed-table-and-chairs arrangements. In a situation such as this, group participants by having them swivel their chairs to work with those behind them.

◆ *Organization/function grouping:* Group learners from the same organization or functional area within an organization. This can enhance application to the job. Alternatively, if the course content is sensitive, consider not having them in the same group.

◆ *Organizational level grouping:* Mix the learners so that you have management, professional, and administrative people in a group. Alternatively, you may want to have homogeneous groups to deal with specific company issues.

Handout 6–24
Sequencing Learning Activities and Giving Feedback (Complete)

Sequence

The sequence of learning activities should vary in pace, intensity, and level of learner involvement. This is useful not only in meeting the needs of varied learning styles, but also in helping the learners pace themselves so they can "rest" during less intense activities. For example, it would *not* be advisable to have the following lesson sequence:

1. role play
2. structured exercise
3. application activity
4. debriefing discussion.

You, and they, would be exhausted! A better example of sequence is

1. interactive lecture
2. structured exercise
3. discussion
4. application
5. debriefing discussion.

Adding in the lecture and discussion provides rest stops between more intense activities.

Sequencing Tips

- ◆ Build the learners' interest with easy content followed by more demanding content.
- ◆ Sequence activities so that the learners master each subskill all the way through before putting those skills together in a comprehensive skill practice.
- ◆ Always have a debriefing discussion when an activity is over; it solidifies the content for the learners, and provides a "rest" in the lesson sequence.

Providing Feedback to Learners

- ◆ A key ingredient in sequencing is in deciding when and how to provide feedback to the learners.
- ◆ When a learner responds during a discussion, you want to affirm that learner and, if you can, affirm the given response. You may say things such as, "That's good" or "Great response" or "I like that. Anyone else have a comment?"
- ◆ In other cases, the respondent may provide a superficial answer, and you want more depth. In that case, you may say something along the lines of "Yes, now can you tell me more?" or "OK, now take me deeper into what you have in mind," or "Great start.

continued on next page

Handout 6–24, continued

Sequencing Learning Activities and Giving Feedback (Complete)

What else can we say about that?" Although you're affirming, you're also letting the learner know that there is more learning to be gained from the question.

◆ A more difficult situation occurs when the learner's response is not correct. This is where you cannot afford to agree. Part of giving feedback is to indicate when a response is incorrect. Yes, you still want to affirm the learner, but not the incorrect answer. In this case, you may reply, "I understand what you're saying, but that relates more to . . . " or you might paraphrase the response and say, "That relates more to . . . than the current subject." By all means, be tactful, but don't accept answers that are superficial, incomplete, or wrong. Your role is to help the participants learn.

◆ Tests and assessments also are ways to provide immediate feedback to participants. These can be written or oral. Because they're used for development, it's important that you go over the tests and explain why wrong answers are wrong. This not only gives feedback—it also reinforces content.

◆ Debriefings provide great opportunities to give feedback to learners, both during learning activities and, especially, after an activity is complete. The debriefing is the opportunity for you to summarize the lessons learned, to reinforce the content, and to support transfer.

Handout 6–25
Using Media (Complete)

Flipcharts and Easels

When to use

- ◆ At informal learning events
- ◆ To generate materials or items on the spot

Tips

- ◆ Make your writing legible and large (six lines per page, letters two inches high).
- ◆ Vary the colors.
- ◆ Write notes to yourself in light pencil on the pages.
- ◆ "Touch, turn, talk"—write on the chart (and don't talk *to* the chart while writing), turn, then speak.

Pluses and minuses

- + Informality creates a comfortable environment.
- – These don't work well in large rooms; they can't be seen by learners who are more than 30 feet away.

Overhead Transparencies

When to use

- ◆ Blank transparencies can be used to generate material and items on the spot
- ◆ When instructing from multiple sites

Tips

- ◆ Talk to learners, not to the glass in front of you or the screen behind you.
- ◆ Point out transparency items on the glass, not on the screen behind you.
- ◆ Turn off the projector when you're finished with the content on that transparency and you want to direct attention elsewhere, also when changing transparencies to avoid glare.
- ◆ Revelation technique: place a piece of paper under the transparency and slide it slowly to reveal one item at a time.

Pluses and minuses

- + These are very useful for learning events you'll facilitate multiple times.
- – They need fairly low room light for good visibility.

Whiteboards

When to use

- ◆ At informal learning events
- ◆ To generate material or brainstorm items on the spot

continued on next page

Handout 6–25, continued
Using Media (Complete)

Tips

- ◆ Write headings on the board to keep your talk organized.
- ◆ Use it to jot notes during a discussion.
- ◆ Use dry-erase markers.

Pluses and minuses

- + Learners can use them for activities and presentations.
- + If you have enough boards, a record of progress can be kept throughout the learning event.
- – You can't move the board around the room or to another area.

PowerPoint Slides, Digital Presentations, or Photographic Slides
When to use

- ◆ At formal learning events
- ◆ Good for learning events you'll facilitate multiple times

Tips

- ◆ Use large, sans serif fonts.
- ◆ Incorporate graphics.
- ◆ Talk to learners, not to the screen behind you.
- ◆ Don't use these media too often or too much.

Pluses and minuses

- + These can be eye-catching and very visual.
- – Technology can break down.

Videos and DVDs
When to use

- ◆ Good for behavioral modeling (watch someone doing right or wrong)
- ◆ During situation or case analysis

Tips

- ◆ Make sure there are enough monitors for all to see.
- ◆ Stop to discuss after a maximum of 15 minutes; then start up again.
- ◆ Be sure settings and clothing in film are not too dated; this could be distracting.

Pluses and minuses

- + These provide excellent media variety.
- – They can be used for too long ("the electronic babysitter").

continued on next page

Handout 6–25, continued

Using Media (Complete)

Written Materials

When to use

- You want learners to have references and takeaways
- The learners must work alone

Tips

- Use colors and graphics as discussed above.
- Provide white space for note taking.
- Distribute only as they are needed so learners don't read ahead.
- You can make hard copies of PowerPoint and digital presentations for later reference.

Pluses and minuses

+ These materials give more detailed information for later reference.

– They don't resonate with auditory learners.

Props and Objects

When to use

- You want to make a point especially memorable

Tips

- Use your imagination.
- Use props that are natural and comfortable for you.
- Take advantage of your own special talents.
- Make sure the illustration or analogy is accurate and easily understood.

Pluses and minuses

+ They help the learners remember the presentation, or specific points in it.
– They may not be well received by the participants if they're perceived as too hokey.

Source: Adapted with permission from Deborah Davis Tobey and Deb Tobey LLC, 2003.

Handout 6–26

Physical Presentation Tips (Complete)

Voice

- ◆ Enunciate and speak clearly,
- ◆ Pause. Don't be afraid of dead air—your audience needs time to think.
- ◆ Relax your mouth and jaw.
- ◆ Vary inflection and pitch—avoid monotone.
- ◆ Project (or use a microphone)!
- ◆ Don't talk too fast (the audience can't understand you and you appear nervous) or too slow (this causes the audience's energy to droop).

Nonverbal behaviors

- ◆ Hold eye contact with an individual for a few seconds, then look away. Don't "bore a hole" into another person's forehead.
- ◆ Exhibit animated facial expressions.
- ◆ Smile and show interest.
- ◆ When upset, maintain a neutral facial expression.

Body language

- ◆ Use gestures appropriately. Using some lends energy and animation but too much motion makes you appear nervous.
- ◆ Move around the room; generate energy.
- ◆ Don't be tied to a lectern, table, or LCD because you can't attend to the learners or move around.

Posture

- ◆ Keep feet flat on the floor.
- ◆ Shoulders should be straight and facing front.
- ◆ Keep hands below shoulders; don't mess with clothing, hair, jewelry, and so on.
- ◆ During low-energy times of day, don't lean on furniture; the audience's energy will also droop.

Dress and appearance

- ◆ Clean
- ◆ Combed
- ◆ Pressed
- ◆ Not too faddish
- ◆ Dress one level above the audience. If learners are in work clothes, wear business casual. If they're in business casual, wear dressy business casual. If they're in jackets, wear a suit. This shows respect for the audience in that you made an effort in your appearance, but you're not placing yourself "above" them.

Handout 6–27

Checklist for Room Setup

Instructions: Use this handout as a checklist. After you have considered these factors and made decisions around them, put a check (√) in the corresponding box.

√	FACTOR	ASPECTS TO CONSIDER
☐	The number of participants	This gives you initial insight into the size of room required for the learning activity.
☐	The type of learning activities	Group activities require rounds, team tables, or breakout rooms. If you have breakout rooms, you may use a smaller main room. If all group work is to be done at team tables, you'll need a larger training room. Be sure that participants don't have you at their backs.
☐	The number of teams	The more teams, the more breakout rooms, or the larger the training room required.
☐	The number of members on each team	The more members on a team, the larger the breakout room or team tables will have to be. In many cases, the larger the team, the more difficult it is to have an environment that's conducive to learning.
☐	Physical limitations of the space	Narrow versus wide floor plans, pillars, folding doors, irregular walls, wall surfaces for hanging visuals, and the ratio of windows to wall space can influence the types of activities, the number of individuals, and the presentation styles that can be accommodated in any space. Windows not only provide a distraction; they also let in light, which could negatively affect the media you plan to use.
☐	Required equipment for the facilitator and teams	Each team will need a flipchart, not a whiteboard. The facilitator may need two flipcharts, media equipment, and a table for supplies. A fixed screen may be at the front or in the corner. Make it easy for participants to view the media. Corner screens can provide greater visibility, up to a point. Depending on how far away and the angle, learners seated on the same side as the screen may have some trouble seeing it. If possible, your screen should hang at a slant—

continued on next page

Handout 6–27, continued

Checklist for Room Setup

√	FACTOR	ASPECTS TO CONSIDER
		that is, the top of the screen should hang a few inches farther away from the wall than the bottom portion. This technique eliminates the *keystone effect*, which occurs when a screen hangs exactly parallel to the wall behind it and the image is distorted to look bigger at the top than at the bottom. Using a remote control gives you freedom of movement.
☐	Your personal space	Given windows, room shape, and physical limitations, decide where you will situate the front of the room.
☐	Facilitation delivery style: podium, lectern, or open	An open style requires just a front table to hold your materials and a side table for handouts. Podiums and lecterns form barriers between you and the participants, and they limit your ability to move around. They're fine for lectures or presentations, but not for facilitating learning experiences.
☐	Room temperature	Check the room thermostat and adjust it accordingly; the more bodies in the room, the higher the temperature will climb. If the temperature is centrally controlled, find out how to make adjustments before the program begins. Start with a room that's a little too cool.
☐	Peripheral materials and methods	Posters on the wall, handouts on the table, and portfolios or writing tablets make the room seem less sterile and give arriving learners something to look at and talk about. Provide nametags or name tent cards so the learners can identify themselves for you and for each other. If your course includes equipment or jobsite materials, having samples of those on the tables enhances learning.
☐	Refreshments	Consider having a variety of hot and cold drinks on hand, and frequently replenish them. Provide an assortment of pastries, bagels, and fruits. Remember that not everyone can tolerate processed sugar, so if you place candies on the tables, be sure you include some that are sugar-free.

Handout 6–28
Sample Room Layouts

A. Room set up in rounds, using round tables

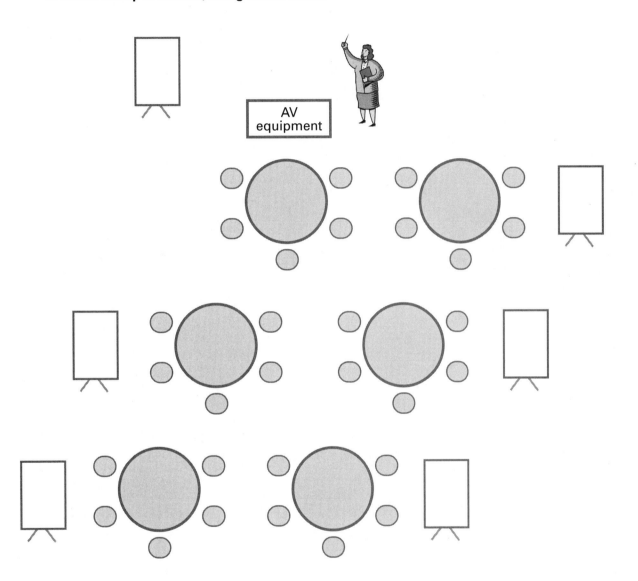

The facilitator shares the flipchart at the front with a group.

continued on next page

Handout 6–28, continued

Sample Room Layouts

B. Room set up in rounds, using rectangular tables

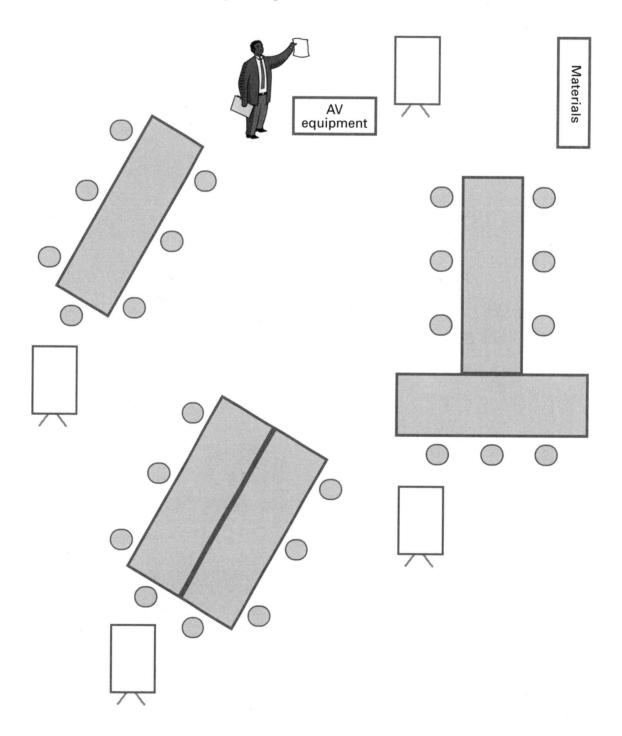

continued on next page

Handout 6–28, continued

Sample Room Layouts

C. U-shaped setup

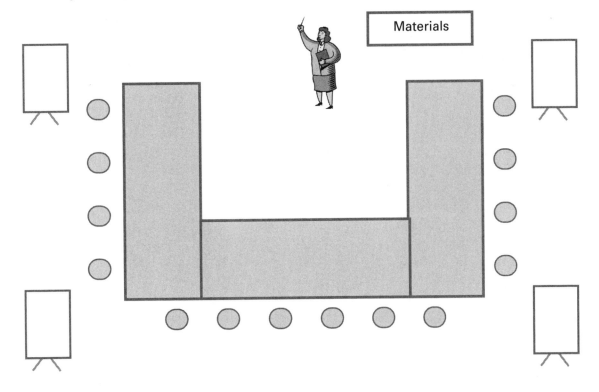

The tables forming the U are set up in the center of
the room so that there is space for small groups to
pull their chairs away from the tables and work
together around the periphery of the U.

continued on next page

Handout 6–28, continued
Sample Room Layouts

D. Chevron setup

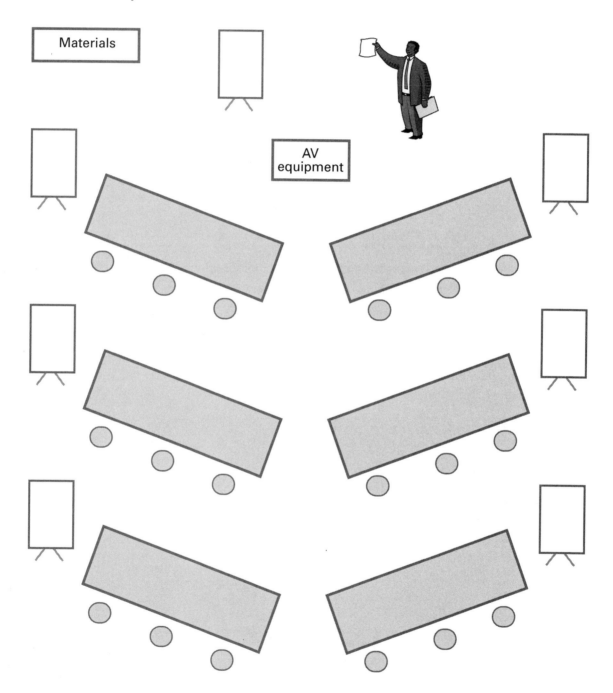

continued on next page

Handout 6–28, continued
Sample Room Layouts

E. Hybrid or fishbone setup

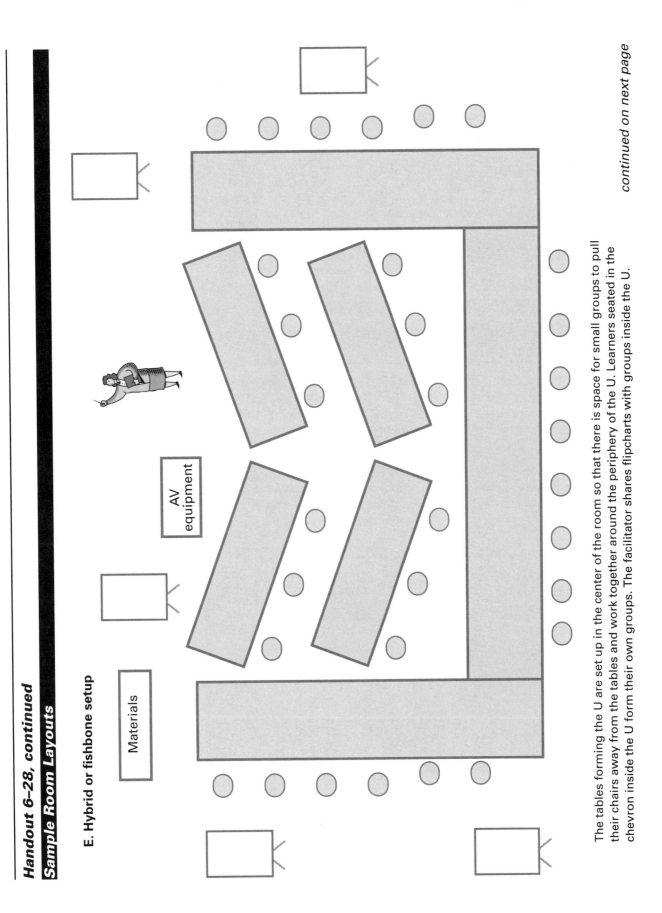

The tables forming the U are set up in the center of the room so that there is space for small groups to pull their chairs away from the tables and work together around the periphery of the U. Learners seated in the chevron inside the U form their own groups. The facilitator shares flipcharts with groups inside the U.

continued on next page

Handout 6–28, continued
Sample Room Layouts

F. Classroom setup

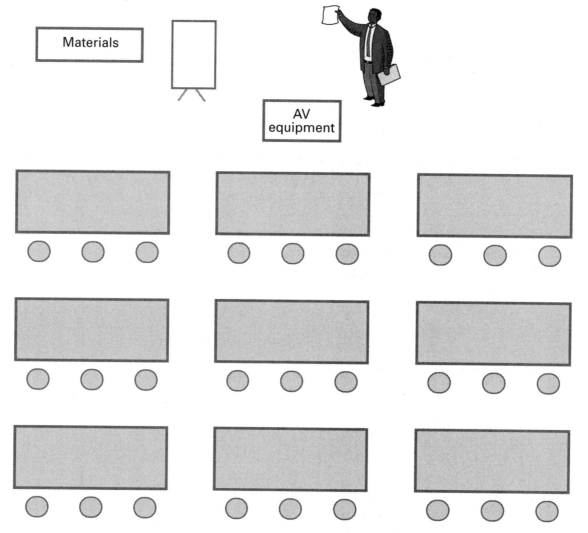

continued on next page

Handout 6–28, continued

Sample Room Layouts

G. Conference setup, using oblong table

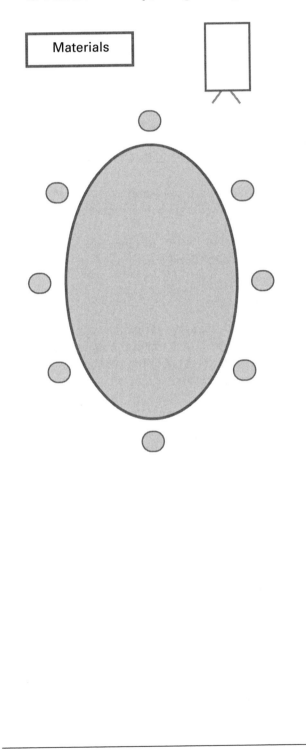

H. Conference setup, using rectangular table

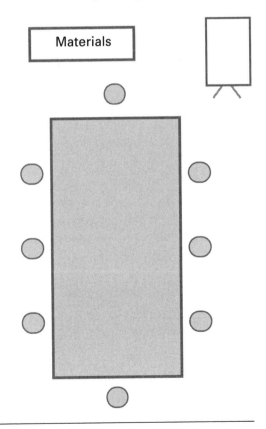

Handout 6–29

Room Setup Considerations

The number of participants

◆ This gives you initial insight into the size of room you will need for the learning activity.

The type of learning activities

◆ Group activities require rounds, team tables, or breakout rooms. If you have breakout rooms, you may use a smaller main room. If all group work is to be done at team tables, you'll need a larger training room to accommodate the tables. Be sure that participants don't have you at their backs.

The number of teams

◆ The more teams, the more breakout rooms or the larger the training room required.

The number of members on each team

◆ The more members on a team, the larger the breakout room or team tables you'll need. In many cases, the larger the team, the more difficult it is to have an environment that's conducive to learning.

Physical limitations of the space

◆ Narrow versus wide floor plans, pillars, folding doors, irregular walls, wall surfaces for hanging visuals, and the ratio of windows to wall space affect the activities, the number and placement of people, and the presentation styles that can be accommodated in any room. Windows not only provide a distraction; they also let in light, which could negatively affect the media you plan to use.

Required equipment for the facilitator and teams

◆ Each team will need a flipchart, not a whiteboard. The facilitator may need two flipcharts, media equipment, and a table for supplies.

◆ A fixed screen may be at the front or in the corner. Make it easy for participants to view the media.

◆ Corner screens can provide greater visibility—to a point. Depending on how far away and the angle at which the screen is set, learners seated on the same side as the screen may have some trouble seeing it.

◆ If possible, your screen should hang at a slant; that is, the top of the screen should hang a few inches closer to the wall than the bottom portion. This technique eliminates the keystone effect.

◆ Using a remote control for the materials you're displaying on the screen gives you freedom of movement.

Your personal space

◆ Given windows, room shape, and physical space limitations, decide where you want to situate the front of the room.

continued on next page

Handout 6–29, continued
Room Setup Considerations

Facilitation delivery style—podium, lectern, or open

◆ An open style requires only a front table to hold your materials and a side table for handouts. Podiums and lecterns form barriers between you and the participants and they limit your ability to move around. They're fine for lectures or presentations, but not for facilitating learning experiences.

Room temperature

◆ Check the room thermostat and adjust it accordingly; the more bodies in the room, the higher the temperature will become. If the temperature is centrally controlled, find out how to make adjustments before the program begins. Start with a room that's a little cooler than you want it to be when the session is under way.

Peripheral materials and methods

◆ Posters on the wall, handouts on the table, and portfolios or writing tablets make the room seem less sterile and give arriving learners something to look at and talk about. Provide nametags or name tent cards so the learners can identify themselves for you and for each other. If your course includes equipment or jobsite materials, having samples of those on the tables enhances learning.

Refreshments

◆ Consider having a variety of hot and cold drinks on hand; and frequently replenish them. Provide a combination of pastries, bagels, and fruits.

Learner seating arrangements

◆ *Rounds or small groups (see illustrations A and B in Handout 6–28):* This is a setup that uses multiple round tables at which learners are seated; despite the name, you can also set up rectangular tables as small groups. The rounds are placed throughout the room for maximum visibility. The facilitator is at the front with whatever tables are required for audiovisual equipment and materials. Flipcharts can be placed beside the rounds for group work. Flipcharts for the center rounds will be placed at the side of the room. If you're using small rectangular tables, you can put two tables together for added seating and workspace. You also might develop the T-effect by placing two tables at a 90-degree angle to each other.

◆ *U-shaped setup (see illustration C in Handout 6–28):* This setup has two sets of tables parallel to each other, making two sides of the U, and another set of tables placed at 90 degrees to the parallel tables. The tables joining the two sides of the U should be placed toward the back of the room. The inside of the U is open. There may be a facilitator's table at the front, but it doesn't close the space. The number of tables in a U-shaped setup depends on three factors: (a) the total number of learners (the optimum usually is 12–18), (b) the number of learners who can be seated comfortably at an individual table, and (c) the overall size of the room.

◆ *Chevron setup (see illustration D in Handout 6–28):* This setup is like a classroom setup with rounds, except that the tables are rectangular. Rows of tables placed at an

continued on next page

Handout 6–29, continued

Room Setup Considerations

angle are aligned one in front of the other, forming a V-shape with an aisle between the rows.

- *Hybrid or fishbone setup (see illustration E in Handout 6–28):* This setup combines the U and chevron setups. If the room is large enough to accommodate the breadth of the required tables, it's used when there are too many learners to be seated in a U. In this setup, you set the U and then develop the chevron within the U.

- *Classroom setup (see illustration F in Handout 6–28):* The classroom configuration has been the traditional setup for the last century. Rows of tables and chairs all face the facilitator, who stands at the front. Usually, the facilitator works from a table with a side table for materials.

- *Conference setup (see illustrations G and H in Handout 6–28):* The conference setup involves several learners sitting around a conference table. The table's shape can be oblong or rectangular. The facilitator has the option of sitting at the head (thus indicating a leadership position), or joining the group by sitting in another seat.

Handout 6–30
Tips for Room Setup

- Always arrive at least an hour early on the first day. This allows time to check the room and have it set or reset under your guidance.
- If necessary, make additional changes at lunch or before the start of the next day.
- Verify that the room can accommodate your desired setup. If not, change rooms.
- If you use breakout rooms, make sure they have the required equipment and supplies and are in close proximity to your main room.
- Ensure the room can accommodate all forms of media.
- Don't use a room with columns.
- Determine the amount of wall space available for posting required flipchart work and wallboards or posters.
- If you have windows, be sure you can close some blinds or drapes if sun conditions or media warrant.
- Be sure the room is not located in a high-traffic area.
- Make certain you can secure the room to protect valuables during breaks.
- If the course covers several days, be sure that crews cleaning the space between sessions don't throw out the work that has been done.

Handout 6–31

Strategies for Dealing with Disruptive Behavior

Instructions: In the first column is a list of learner disruptive behaviors that you are likely to encounter during your course. Devise strategies or actions to address each disruptive behavior and record them in the second column.

LEARNER'S DISRUPTIVE BEHAVIOR	FACILITATOR STRATEGIES OR ACTIONS TO ADDRESS DISRUPTIVE BEHAVIOR
Engages in side conversation	
Talks too much; monopolizes the discussion	
Complains; is negative about the class or organization	
Daydreams; is not really "in the class"	
Heckles the facilitator	
Challenges the facilitator on content or technique; is a know-it-all	
Tells jokes or clowns around at inappropriate times	
Makes an inappropriate remark (such as a sexist or racist one)	
Does other work, reads the newspaper, or takes/makes cell phone calls	
Is silent; doesn't participate verbally	
Is withdrawn from the group—interpersonally, physically, or both	
Goes off on a tangent; misses the point	

Handout 6–32

Recognizing and Responding to Disruptive Learner Behavior

WHAT HAPPENS IN THE ROOM	WHAT THE FACILITATOR THINKS AND DOES
Learner exhibits disruptive behavior (example: doing other things during the class and not paying attention) based on unknown personal agenda.	This person is doing other work, reading the newspaper, working with his Blackberry, or whatever.
Facilitator's own personal agenda is triggered.	That learner is ignoring me! I'm embarrassed because everyone sees that I'm being ignored. I want to embarrass and punish this person.
Facilitator realizes that his or her personal agenda has been triggered and recognizes the behaviors that could be created out of that personal agenda.	I could direct an unexpected question or remark to this person to catch him or her off guard in front of the rest of the class. But that learner's behavior isn't about me, it's about his needs. What could be the most probable agenda?
Facilitator identifies learner's probable personal agenda.	This learner's probably bored. He's more advanced in this subject than the other learners
Facilitator mentally reiterates professional agenda.	I must continue to make learning happen.
Facilitator chooses to act on professional rather than on personal agenda. She or he chooses behaviors that meet the learner's agenda. By doing this, the disruptive behavior is extinguished and the learning continues	*Possible Actions:* Ask the learner to do a short presentation about his experience; ask him to coach another learner who's very inexperienced; speak to the learner during a break and point out that he doesn't appear to be engaged. Ask, What can I do to meet those needs?

Handout 6–33

Recommended Strategies to Deal with Disruptive Behaviors

LEARNER'S DISRUPTIVE BEHAVIOR	FACILITATOR STRATEGIES OR ACTIONS THAT MEET THE LEARNER'S AGENDA AND CONTINUE THE LEARNING
Engages in side conversation	◆ Behave as if you know the side conversation is class related, and ask the participants to add their thoughts. ◆ If you're lecturing or leading a discussion, slowly move into the part of the room where the disrupters are; continue the lecture or discussion, and don't look at them as you continue. ◆ Change the pace of the activity; do something dynamic (for instance, have participants use flipcharts or put them into small group discussions). ◆ Re-form the groups, separating the disrupters. ◆ At the start of the next session, revisit the class norms and ground rules.
Talks too much; monopolizes discussion	◆ If the learner is on the subject, begin talking with him or her and summarize the learner's point. Then turn to others and invite their participation: "What does everyone else think?" ◆ Avoid making eye contact with the disrupter for a while. ◆ If he or she is off target, say, "Great point, but it's beyond the scope of our class. . . . Let's talk about this together outside of class." ◆ Put the learner's issue on a Parking Lot flipchart for later discussion. ◆ Change the pace of the activity and have participants do solo work for a short time.
Complains; is negative about the class or organization	◆ Ask if others feel the same way. If they don't, then offer to assist or listen to the disrupter during a break. ◆ If others do feel the same way, facilitate a "productive tangent." ◆ Acknowledge the complaint, then turn group discussion to strategizing how to overcome it. ◆ Write the issue on the Parking Lot flipchart. ◆ If the complaint is valid, incorporate it into the action planning to have the learner address the issue.
Daydreams; is not really "in the class"	◆ Change the current activity to make it more dynamic or involving. ◆ If the daydreaming is organization related and more than one person is doing it, acknowledge it and allow a short discussion; then move on.

Behavior	Response
Heckles the facilitator	◆ Talk to the disruptive learner privately during a break and ask how the class could be better meeting his or her needs. ◆ Frequently link content to the job.
	◆ Give the learner your attention in a learning-oriented way rather than encouraging the heckling. ◆ Change the activity so that the participants are interacting with each other rather than with you. ◆ If the heckling continues, talk privately with the person. Ask if the class is meeting her or his needs. If not, or if she or he doesn't want to be there, acknowledge and support that within the constraints of the program. If the disruptions continue, send the disrupter back to the job.
Challenges the facilitator on content or technique; is a know-it-all	◆ Give the person the spotlight for a few minutes. ◆ Turn the exchange into a discussion by implying that there are multiple points of view and all should be addressed. Ask for other opinions from the rest of the group.
Tells jokes or clowns around at inappropriate times	◆ Give the learner attention by reengaging him or her in the content without acknowledging the joking behavior. ◆ If the jokes are intended to relieve tension, help the group by bringing up the discomfort directly or put them in small groups so they can discuss more comfortably. ◆ When a joke is funny and told at the right time, laugh!
Makes an inappropriate remark (such as a sexist or racist one)	◆ Deal with it in front of the group; it can't be ignored. First, give her or him a chance to retract: "I'm sure you didn't mean that the way it sounded...." If she or he does retract, move on. If the person does not retract, say, "That view isn't in keeping with the values of our organization, and we can't have any more of that." Speak with the person during break, and report the behavior to her or his manager, if necessary. Revisit norms and ground rules concerning respect for others.
Does other work, reads the newspaper, or takes/makes cell phone calls	◆ Speak to the disruptive learner during a break and point out that his or her behavior leads you to believe the class is not meeting his or her needs. Ask how the class can better serve those needs, and try to do that. ◆ Acknowledge the pressure. Negotiate with the participant to appear engaged so that his or her behavior doesn't affect the rest of the group.

continued on next page

Handout 6–33, continued

Recommended Strategies to Deal with Disruptive Behaviors

LEARNER'S DISRUPTIVE BEHAVIOR	FACILITATOR STRATEGIES OR ACTIONS THAT MEET THE LEARNER'S AGENDA AND CONTINUE THE LEARNING
Is silent; doesn't participate verbally	◆ Offer the opportunity to attend another session at a time that would be less pressured. ◆ Create opportunities for the learner to participate safely in pairs or small groups. ◆ Pace some activities so there is time for reflection before participants discuss and share opinions. ◆ If you can tell by the learner's body language that she or he is engaged, listening, reacting, and thinking, consider simply leaving that learner alone.
Is withdrawn from the group—interpersonally, physically, or both	◆ Ask the person at the next break what is going on and how you can help. Deal with the issue accordingly after that. ◆ Have small groups rotate the persons presenting. ◆ Encourage groups to have all members actively involved.
Goes off on a tangent; misses the point	◆ Find one thing to agree with in what the learner has said. ◆ Affirm and compliment his or her effort to stay engaged with the content. ◆ Say, "That would be a logical assumption; however, the truth is…. " If his or her effort is contrived to see what you'll do, the most effective behavior is to address the content of the question rather than to take the bait.

Source: Adapted with permission from Deborah Davis Tobey and Deb Tobey LLC, 2003.

Handout 6-34

A Comprehensive Response for Dealing with Disruptive Behaviors

LEARNER'S DISRUPTIVE BEHAVIOR	STEP 1: FACILITATOR'S PERSONAL AGENDA IS TRIGGERED	STEP 2: FACILITATOR RECOGNIZES HIS OR HER PERSONAL AGENDA AND POTENTIAL BEHAVIORS, BUT CHOOSES NOT TO ACT ON IT	STEP 3: FACILITATOR IDENTIFIES LEARNER'S PROBABLE PERSONAL AGENDA	STEP 4: FACILITATOR MENTALLY REITERATES PROFESSIONAL AGENDA	STEP 5: FACILITATOR CHOOSES TO ACT ON PROFESSIONAL AGENDA, WITH BEHAVIORS THAT MEET THE LEARNER'S AGENDA
Has side conversation(s)	• Thinks, "They are being disrespectful and rude. I want to treat them the same way so they see what it feels like."	• Wants to ask, "Do you two have something to share?" • Wants to ask the class a question; then direct the question to one of the disrupters to catch her or him off guard.	• Guesses that they're talking about something relevant to the class. • Figures they're talking about something relevant to work, but not to the class. • Assumes the disrupters aren't engaged in the class; that they're talking to keep themselves awake.	• Thinks, "I must continue to make learning happen."	• Behaves as if she "knows" the side conversation is class-related, and asks them to add their thoughts. In the event that the side conversation actually was class-related, the facilitator has reinforced their involvement and participation. • If she is lecturing or leading a discussion, the facilitator slowly moves into the part of the room where the disrupters are seated; she continues the lecture or discussion, and doesn't look at them. (This only works if the facilitator has already established a habit of moving around the room.) • The facilitator changes the pace of the activity; does something dynamic (for instance, has participants create flipchart presentations or puts them in small group discussions). • The facilitator reforms groups by counting off—making sure the disrupters are separated. • At the start of the next session, she again

continued on next page

Handout 6-34, continued

A Comprehensive Response for Dealing with Disruptive Behaviors

LEARNER'S DISRUPTIVE BEHAVIOR	STEP 1: FACILITATOR'S PERSONAL AGENDA IS TRIGGERED	STEP 2: FACILITATOR RECOGNIZES HIS OR HER PERSONAL AGENDA AND POTENTIAL BEHAVIORS, BUT CHOOSES NOT TO ACT ON IT	STEP 3: FACILITATOR IDENTIFIES LEARNER'S PROBABLE PERSONAL AGENDA	STEP 4: FACILITATOR MENTALLY REITERATES PROFESSIONAL AGENDA	STEP 5: FACILITATOR CHOOSES TO ACT ON PROFESSIONAL AGENDA, WITH BEHAVIORS THAT MEET THE LEARNER'S AGENDA
					◆ goes over the class norms and ground rules.
Talks too much; monopolizes discussion	◆ Thinks, "I'm frustrated; I wish this person would shut up—and stay that way."	◆ Wants to do anything that shuts the person down in a mean or embarrassing way: a joke, labeling him as a talker, rolling eyes, and so on. ◆ Wants to collude in some way with the group if members are rolling eyes or showing other signs of exasperation.	◆ Thinks the disrupter wants attention. ◆ Guesses that he's a person who thinks out loud. ◆ Assumes he wants to demonstrate knowledge or expertise.	◆ Thinks, "I must continue to make learning happen."	◆ If the disrupter is on the subject, the facilitator begins talking with her or him and summarizes the point. Then turns to others and invites their participation: "What does everyone else think?" ◆ Avoids eye contact with the disrupter for a while. ◆ If the disrupter is off target, the facilitator says, "Great point, but it's beyond the scope of our class. . . . Let's talk about this together—or outside of class." ◆ The facilitator puts the issue on a Parking Lot flipchart (to be dealt with at the proper time). ◆ Changes the pace of the activity and asks participants to do solo work for a short while.
Complains; is negative about the class or organization	◆ Thinks, "What a whiner! This person needs to shut up before she brings the whole group down and I have to bring them back up somehow."	◆ Wants to argue with her. ◆ Wants to cut her off before she can finish her thought. ◆ Would like to say, "Well, there's nothing	◆ Guesses the person doesn't want to be there, has other things on her mind that are more important for her. ◆ Assumes she wants	◆ Thinks, "I must continue to make learning happen."	◆ The facilitator asks if others feel the same way. If they don't, then he offers to assist and/or listen to the disrupter during a break. ◆ If others do feel the

continued on next page

	Thinks	Wants/Does	Facilitator Response
		"...we can do about that." Wants not to acknowledge the speaker and/or the complaint.	same way, the facilitator might have a productive tangent to deal with (see the section about adjusting on the fly). Negative feelings and complaints (on the part of the majority of the group) must be acknowledged and handled, or they simply will fester and learning won't happen. • The facilitator acknowledges the complaint; then turns the group discussion to strategizing how to overcome it. • Puts the issue in the Parking Lot. • If the complaint is valid, the facilitator incorporates it into the action planning to have the learner address the issue.
		her complaint to be acknowledged.	
Daydreams; is not "in the class"	Thinks, "This person is being rude to me, and is influencing others to drift off. I'm embarrassed so I want to embarrass him."	• Wants to call on him unexpectedly • Would like to joke: "Earth to John. Come in, John." • Would like to introduce an unexpected game or test activity: "Let's see who's been paying attention"—in effect, punishing the whole class.	• Guesses he's not engaged in the class and would rather be somewhere else. • Assumes the content isn't relevant to the disrupter. • Figures the disrupter thinks this class is just part of another initiative that will pass.
	Thinks, "I must continue to make learning happen."		• The facilitator changes the current activity to make it more dynamic and involving. For example, if the class is engaged in small group discussions, she asks learners to produce a flipchart showing their work. • If the daydreaming is organization related and more than one person is doing it (for example, everyone's minds are on the current layoff situation), the facilitator acknowledges the distraction and prompts a short

Handout 6-34, continued

A Comprehensive Response for Dealing with Disruptive Behaviors

LEARNER'S DISRUPTIVE BEHAVIOR	STEP 1: FACILITATOR'S PERSONAL AGENDA IS TRIGGERED	STEP 2: FACILITATOR RECOGNIZES HIS OR HER PERSONAL AGENDA AND POTENTIAL BEHAVIORS, BUT CHOOSES NOT TO ACT ON IT	STEP 3: FACILITATOR IDENTIFIES LEARNER'S PROBABLE PERSONAL AGENDA	STEP 4: FACILITATOR MENTALLY REITERATES PROFESSIONAL AGENDA	STEP 5: FACILITATOR CHOOSES TO ACT ON PROFESSIONAL AGENDA, WITH BEHAVIORS THAT MEET THE LEARNER'S AGENDA
					discussion; then the class moves on. • The facilitator speaks privately with the disrupter during a break; she asks how the class could better meet his needs. • The facilitator frequently links content to the job.
Heckles the facilitator	• Thinks, "Smart aleck! I want to put her down like she's putting me down."	• Wants to continue to "volley" with the heckler as the rest of the group watches. • Would like to label the behavior in front of the group: "Oh, so we have a smart aleck in our midst!"	• Believes the disrupter wants attention. • Figures she's just a clown who thinks the heckling is funny, not rude. • Assumes she doesn't want to be there. • Fears the joker wants to destroy the facilitator's credibility.	• Thinks, "I must continue to make learning happen."	• The facilitator gives the disrupter attention in a learning-oriented way rather than in a way that encourages the heckling: "Mary, you clearly have some background in this area; would you share your thoughts with the rest of the group?" • The facilitator changes the activity so that the participants are interacting with each other rather than with the facilitator. • If the heckling continues, the facilitator talks privately with the heckler, asking if the class is meeting her needs. If not, or if she doesn't want to be there, the facilitator acknowledges and supports that within the constraints of the

Behavior					
					program. If the heckling continues, he sends her back to the job.
Challenges the facilitator on content or technique; is a know-it-all	Thinks, "I'm the expert; I'm right. This person is hurting my credibility and should not be allowed to challenge me."	Wants to say, "That may be true in your experience, but we're not talking about that in here" (meaning: your experience is not relevant). Wants to ignore the person's comments.	Guesses the disrupter wants to be recognized for his own expertise. Thinks he wants some of the spotlight. Fears he wants to destroy the facilitator's credibility.	Thinks, "I must continue to make learning happen."	The facilitator gives the person the spotlight for a few minutes, believing that his expertise will add to the learning. (Remember, the facilitator's credibility comes from her or his ability as a facilitator and from personal expertise.) The facilitator turns the exchange into a discussion by implying that there are multiple points of view and all should be addressed. He asks for other opinions from the rest of the group.
Tells jokes or clowns around at inappropriate times	Thinks, "That's funny!" or "That's not funny!"	Is inclined to support the behavior by laughing or continuing to banter. Wants to shut the person down by embarrassing her.	Believes the disrupter wants attention. Guesses she may be uncomfortable with the subject, so is making jokes to help herself handle it. Thinks she's bored and wants to liven things up.	Thinks, "I must continue to make learning happen."	The facilitator gives the disrupter attention by re-engaging her with the content but without acknowledging the joking behavior. If discomfort with the subject is apparent in more group members, then the jokes are intended to relieve tension. In such a case, the facilitator helps the group by bringing up the discomfort directly, or puts the class members in small groups so they can discuss more comfortably. When a joke is funny and told at the right time, the facilitator laughs!

continued on next page

Handout 6-34, continued
A Comprehensive Response for Dealing with Disruptive Behaviors

LEARNER'S DISRUPTIVE BEHAVIOR	STEP 1: FACILITATOR'S PERSONAL AGENDA IS TRIGGERED	STEP 2: FACILITATOR RECOGNIZES HIS OR HER PERSONAL AGENDA AND POTENTIAL BEHAVIORS, BUT CHOOSES NOT TO ACT ON IT	STEP 3: FACILITATOR IDENTIFIES LEARNER'S PROBABLE PERSONAL AGENDA	STEP 4: FACILITATOR MENTALLY REITERATES PROFESSIONAL AGENDA	STEP 5: FACILITATOR CHOOSES TO ACT ON PROFESSIONAL AGENDA, WITH BEHAVIORS THAT MEET THE LEARNER'S AGENDA
Makes an inappropriate remark (such as a sexist or racist one)	• Thinks, "What an idiot/bigot/sexist! I'm angry! I want to embarrass him!" or "I don't know what to do with this; it's better to do nothing than to make a mistake."	• Would like to react harshly or label the person: "We don't make bigoted remarks in here!" • Wants to ignore the remark or pretend it didn't happen (which implies to participants that the facilitator think it's OK to make such remarks).	• Thinks this person is truly unaware of how the remark sounded. • Fears that the person is fully aware of how the remark sounded and is purposely making the remark anyway.	• Thinks, "I must continue to make learning happen."	• The facilitator must deal with it in front of the group; it cannot be ignored. • The facilitator gives the speaker a chance to retract: "I'm sure you didn't mean that the way it sounded...." If the speaker does retract, the class moves on. (If the disrupter was unaware of the meaning of the remark, he'll suffer enough embarrassment; the facilitator doesn't need to intensify it.) • If the speaker doesn't retract the remark, the facilitator says, in front of the group, "That view is not in keeping with the values of our organization, and we can't have any more of that." The facilitator may need to speak with the person during a break as well—and even report the behavior to the speaker's manager, if necessary. • With the whole group, the facilitator reiterates norms and ground rules of respect for others.

Does other work, reads the newspaper, or takes/makes cell phone calls	• Thinks, "How dare he ignore me! I'm embarrassed. I want to embarrass or punish him."	• Wants to direct an unexpected question or remark to the person to make it obvious that he isn't paying attention.	• Believes the person is not engaged in the class. • Thinks he may feel pressure to be doing other work.	• Thinks, "I must continue to make learning happen."	• The facilitator speaks privately with him during a break and points out that his behavior suggests the class isn't meeting his needs. She asks how the class can better serve those needs, and then she tries to do that in the class setting. • The facilitator acknowledges the pressure, and negotiates with the participant to appear engaged so that his behavior doesn't affect the rest of the group. • She offers him an opportunity to attend another session at a time when the pressure is relieved.
Is silent, doesn't participate verbally	• Thinks, "I want this person to participate (whether she wants to or not!)." • Thinks, "Am I not doing a good job? I *must* engage her."	• Believes it's the facilitator's job to "bring her out of her shell." • Wants to create participation opportunities that will force her to participate.	• Guesses the person is shy and not comfortable speaking up in front of others. • Believes she may be participating by listening and thinking, just not speaking. • Assumes she's primarily a thinker—someone who must observe and reflect on a situation before forming an opinion.	• Thinks, "I must continue to make learning happen."	• The facilitator creates opportunities for her to participate safely—perhaps in pairs or small groups. • The facilitator paces some activities so there is reflection time included (during a break, lunch, or overnight) before participants discuss and share opinions. • If the facilitator can tell by the person's body language that she is engaged, listening, reacting, and thinking, he may consider simply leaving her alone.

continued on next page

Handout 6-34, continued

A Comprehensive Response for Dealing with Disruptive Behaviors

LEARNER'S DISRUPTIVE BEHAVIOR	STEP 1: FACILITATOR'S PERSONAL AGENDA IS TRIGGERED	STEP 2: FACILITATOR RECOGNIZES HIS OR HER PERSONAL AGENDA AND POTENTIAL BEHAVIORS, BUT CHOOSES NOT TO ACT ON IT	STEP 3: FACILITATOR IDENTIFIES LEARNER'S PROBABLE PERSONAL AGENDA	STEP 4: FACILITATOR MENTALLY REITERATES PROFESSIONAL AGENDA	STEP 5: FACILITATOR CHOOSES TO ACT ON PROFESSIONAL AGENDA, WITH BEHAVIORS THAT MEET THE LEARNER'S AGENDA
Withdraws from group interpersonally and/or physically	◆ Thinks, "I must make this man re-engage with the group, no matter what."	◆ Wants to direct questions toward him to force re-engagement. ◆ Wants to make other participants the facilitator's agents and have them attempt to re-engage him.	◆ Guesses this person isn't feeling well. ◆ Thinks he's upset or angry about something that has happened. ◆ Fears he feels excluded or not listened to.	◆ Thinks, "I must continue to make learning happen."	◆ At the next break, the facilitator asks the person what's going on and how she can help. She deals with the issue accordingly after that. ◆ She asks small groups to rotate the people who are presenting the groups' work. ◆ She encourages groups to have all members actively involved.
Goes off on tangent; misses the point	◆ Thinks, "How obtuse can someone be?"	◆ Thinks of making a joke or in some other way belittling her for being wrong.	◆ Thinks the disrupter has misunderstood a point. ◆ Thinks she's on the wrong track. ◆ Thinks she's intentionally being "wrong" to see what the facilitator will do.	◆ Thinks, "I must continue to make learning happen."	◆ If possible, the facilitator finds one thing to agree with in what has been said. ◆ He affirms and compliments her effort to stay engaged with the content, saying, "That would be a logical assumption; however, the truth is...." ◆ If the disrupter's effort is contrived to see what the facilitator will do when provoked, the most effective behavior is to address the content of the question rather than take the disrupter's bait.

Source: Adapted with permission from Deborah Davis Tobey and Deb Tobey LLC, 2003

Handout 6–35
Factors in Adjusting on the Fly

Factor 1—Learner groupings

- The more learner groups, the more time and involvement the activity will take. You can adjust the number of learner groups working together.

- *If you're running short on time:* Adjust the number of groups in an activity in which the learners are to work in pairs or trios to groups of five or six instead. There will be fewer groups to report their work, and the overall activity will take less time.

- *If you have more time than you planned for:* Adjust the number of groups to a larger number of smaller-size groups (such as pairs or trios).

- *If the planned groupings require more involvement than the learners are comfortable with:* When your learners are more shy or reserved than you'd expected, form more and smaller groups.

- *If the planned groupings require less involvement than the learners are comfortable with:* When your learners are more comfortable in large groups and enjoy speaking in front of others, form a few larger groups (or one large group).

Factor 2—Activity logistics

- The more dynamic and complicated its logistics, the more time an activity will take.

- *Types of logistics adjustments:* Number of groups; physical layout; conditions in which the learners will work (will they discuss? work alone, then discuss? move around? stay in the same place?); results they must produce (report, flipchart, presentation, action, and so on); time of day (they need to be more physically active later in the day); and learning styles (is there a preponderance of one style?).

- *The planned logistics support more active involvement than is optimal with a particular group of learners:* You can adjust the logistics for learners who are shy, reserved, novice, sedentary, or at the beginning of a course when they don't know each other. This can be accomplished by (a) having more and smaller-size groups, (b) arranging more "cozy" seating, (c) structuring the activity so they work with the same few people each time or stay in the same place for the duration of the activity, (d) asking for group reporting rather than individual reporting, and (e) having informal rather than more formal reports.

- *If the planned logistics will support less active involvement than is optimal with a particular group of learners:* You can adjust the logistics for learners who are more extroverted, outgoing, experienced, or active in their jobs, and who are at a later point in the course when comfort levels are higher. Accomplish this by having (a) fewer and larger groups, (b) expanded seating arrangements, and (c) a change of partners and locations in the room throughout the activity.

- *If you run short on time:* Adjust downward the complexity of the logistics (for example, have learners appoint a recorder to take notes in his or her group, rather than have the group draw up a flipchart, and have groups report only their "top three" ideas instead of all the ideas they discussed).

continued on next page

Handout 6–35, continued

Factors in Adjusting on the Fly

- ♦ *If more time is available:* Adjust upward the complexity of the logistics (for example, have groups do something physically active, such as build a model, solve a puzzle, make a flipchart, or have them work on assignments in segments and switch groups between segments).

Factor 3—Activity intensity

- ♦ The more learner centered an activity is, the more "intense" an experience it is for the learners. The more intense the activity, the more time it will take and the more "risk" learners will experience.
- ♦ The intensity of activities ranges from lectures (low intensity) to discussions (moderately low intensity) to structured exercises (moderate intensity) to skill practices (high intensity).
- ♦ *If you are short on time:* Adjust the activity intensity downward one step (from a skill practice on the content to a structured bridge activity, from a structured bridge activity to a guided discussion, or from a guided discussion to an interactive lecture).
- ♦ *If more time is available:* Adjust the activity intensity upward one step (from an interactive lecture to a guided discussion, from a guided discussion to a structured bridge activity, from a structured bridge activity to a skill practice).

Factor 4—Preparing ahead of time:

- ♦ Know which content and activities are most critical, and which are "nice to know."
- ♦ Know which activities reinforce skills and link to application on the job.
- ♦ Analyze your content and activities, and identify *what* you will adjust if necessary and *how* you will adjust it.
- ♦ Develop ahead of time the specific changes you'll make in groupings, logistics, or activity intensity should the need arise.
- ♦ Having planned ahead, when you make the actual adjustment in the classroom it will be seamless in the eyes of your learners—and that's what counts.

Handout 6-36

Sample Module Plan—Creating the Climate and Environment for Learning

Approximate Time: 1 hour, 30 minutes

MINUTES	ACTIVITY DESCRIPTION	MATERIALS
10	*The Physical Learning Environment:* Facilitate a guided discussion on considerations for room arrangement.	Handout 6–3: Factors for Room Setup
20	*Learning Preferences:* Facilitate an interactive lecture on learning preferences. Include a discussion with three categories (visual, auditory, kinesthetic) listed on whiteboard, and ask learners to volunteer types of activities.	Handout 6–4: Aligning Learning Activities and Media with Learning Preferences
15	*Learning Styles:* Facilitate an interactive lecture on learning styles.	Handout 6–5: Learning Styles
15	*Learning Activity 5–3: Applying Learning Styles to Facilitation of Learning Experiences:* Divide the group into five subgroups, assigning each group one of the learning styles (achievers, evaluators, networkers, socializers, and observers). Learners work together to identify ways or tecjniques to accommodate the learning needs of an assigned learning style; then they present ideas.	Handout 6–6: Recognizing Learning Styles
25	Debrief the learning activity. As the groups present, facilitate a debriefing guided discussion by augmenting and affirming their answers.	Handout 6–7: Aligning Learning Activities with Learning Preferences and Styles
5	Transition to the next module on types of learning activities.	

Handout 6–37
Advanced Facilitation Skills Training Course Evaluation

Course title: Advanced Facilitation Training   *Facilitator:* _____

Course date: _____   *Course location:* _____

Instructions: The statements below concern specific aspects of this course. Please indicate to what extent you agree with each statement by circling the appropriate number, using the scale below. In the "General" section, respond by placing a checkmark in the appropriate box.

1 = STRONGLY DISAGREE	3 = AGREE
2 = DISAGREE	4 = STRONGLY AGREE

COURSE CONTENT

1. Objectives were clearly explained.   1 2 3 4

2. Stated objectives were met; as the participant, I will be able to
   a. Self-assess knowledge and confidence levels regarding facilitator   1 2 3 4
      competencies and identify those competencies most in need of
      development.
   b. Identify participant learning styles and preferences, and   1 2 3 4
      implement facilitation techniques to accommodate different
      styles and preferences.
   c. Analyze the pros and cons of various types of learning activities.   1 2 3 4
   d. Facilitate a guided discussion.   1 2 3 4
   e. Facilitate a structured bridge activity.   1 2 3 4
   f. Develop strategies to facilitate learning while handling the needs   1 2 3 4
      of disruptive participants.
   g. Develop strategies to adjust on the fly when necessary in a   1 2 3 4
      learning event.
   h. Prepare action plan strategies for facilitation skill practice on   1 2 3 4
      the job.

3. Material was well organized.   1 2 3 4

4. Content is relevant to my job.   1 2 3 4

COURSE METHODOLOGY

5. The following helped me understand the content and achieve the
   objectives:
   a. Handouts   1 2 3 4
   b. Class discussions   1 2 3 4
   c. Individual exercises and activities   1 2 3 4
   d. Small group or team discussions and activities   1 2 3 4
   e. Media (flipcharts, PowerPoint slides, and such)   1 2 3 4

continued on next page

Handout 6–37, continued

Advanced Facilitation Skills Training Course Evaluation

INSTRUCTOR/FACILITATOR

		1	2	3	4
6.	Promoted an environment of learning.	1	2	3	4
7.	Presented content clearly to assist my understanding.	1	2	3	4
8.	Demonstrated knowledge of the subject matter.	1	2	3	4
9.	Effectively provided feedback to participants.	1	2	3	4
10.	Responded well to questions.	1	2	3	4
11.	Presented content in an appropriate sequence.	1	2	3	4
12.	Promoted participant discussion and involvement.	1	2	3	4
13.	Kept the discussion on topic and kept activities on track.	1	2	3	4

ENVIRONMENT/COURSE ADMINISTRATION

		1	2	3	4
14.	The class was free of external distractions.	1	2	3	4
15.	The room was neat and clean.	1	2	3	4
16.	The promotional material accurately represents course content.	1	2	3	4
17.	The registration process is effective.	1	2	3	4

GENERAL

18. Course pace was ☐ too slow ☐ about right ☐ too fast.

19. Overall, I rate this course ☐ poor ☐ fair ☐ good ☐ excellent.

20. I ☐ would ☐ would not recommend this course to my peers.
    Why or why not?

21. These are my suggestions for improving the course:

Thank you for taking the time to share your comments and reactions to your learning experience.

Handout 6–38

Facilitation Skills Training Course Evaluation

Course title: Facilitation Training   *Facilitator:* _____

Course date: _____   *Course location:* _____

Instructions: The statements below concern specific aspects of this course. Please indicate to what extent you agree with each statement by circling the appropriate number, using the scale below. In the "General" section, respond by placing a checkmark in the appropriate box.

1 = STRONGLY DISAGREE	3 = AGREE
2 = DISAGREE	4 = STRONGLY AGREE

COURSE CONTENT

1.	Objectives were clearly explained.	1 2 3 4
2.	Stated objectives were met; as the participant, I will be able to	
	a. Analyze the pros and cons of various types of learning activities.	1 2 3 4
	b. Explain the use of the interactive lecture.	1 2 3 4
	c. Facilitate a guided discussion.	1 2 3 4
	d. Develop strategies to facilitate learning while handling the needs of disruptive participants.	1 2 3 4
	e. Develop strategies to adjust on the fly when necessary in a learning event.	1 2 3 4
	f. Prepare action plan strategies for facilitation skill practice on the job.	1 2 3 4
3.	Material was well organized.	1 2 3 4
4.	Content is relevant to my job.	1 2 3 4

COURSE METHODOLOGY

5.	The following helped me understand the content and achieve the objectives:	
	a. Handouts	1 2 3 4
	b. Class discussions	1 2 3 4
	c. Individual exercises and activities	1 2 3 4
	d. Small group or team discussions and activities	1 2 3 4
	e. Media (flipcharts, PowerPoint slides, and such)	1 2 3 4
6.	Promoted an environment of learning.	1 2 3 4
7.	Presented content clearly to assist my understanding.	1 2 3 4
8.	Demonstrated knowledge of the subject matter.	1 2 3 4
9.	Effectively provided feedback to participants.	1 2 3 4
10.	Responded well to questions.	1 2 3 4

continued on next page

Handout 6–38, continued

Facilitation Skills Training Course Evaluation

INSTRUCTOR/FACILITATOR

		1	2	3	4
11.	Presented content in an appropriate sequence.	1	2	3	4
12.	Promoted participant discussion and involvement.	1	2	3	4
13.	Kept the discussion on topic and kept activities on track.	1	2	3	4

ENVIRONMENT/COURSE ADMINISTRATION

		1	2	3	4
14.	The class was free of external distractions.	1	2	3	4
15.	The room was neat and clean.	1	2	3	4
16.	The promotional material accurately represents course content.	1	2	3	4
17.	The registration process is effective.	1	2	3	4

GENERAL

18. Course pace was ☐ too slow ☐ about right ☐ too fast.

19. Overall, I rate this course ☐ poor ☐ fair ☐ good ☐ excellent.

20. I ☐ would ☐ would not recommend this course to my peers.
    Why or why not?

21. These are my suggestions for improving the course:

Thank you for taking the time to share your comments and reactions to your learning experience.

Handout 6-39
Sample Module Plan—Skill Practices Case Study

Approximate Time: 1 hour, 10 minutes

MINUTES	ACTIVITY DESCRIPTION	MATERIALS
10	*Introduction:* Interactive lecture on the purpose of skill practice.	
25	*Case Study Activity:* ◆ Form three learner groups ◆ Distribute Handout 6–11 ◆ Set up case study with instructions ◆ Pass out Handouts 6–12, 6–13, and 6–14 to small groups ◆ Facilitate and monitor activity (20 minutes)	Handout 6–11: Facilitation Case Study, Handout 6–12: The Case Study, Handout 6–13: Role Play, Handout 6–14: Demonstration and Practice
25	*Group Presentations:* Using a round-robin style, have each group present its answers to the case study questions and then conduct a short debriefing discussion on each handout. ◆ After each group has shared answers to questions 1 through 4 about the driving case study, review with the group Handout 6–12 to ensure all content has been shared. ◆ After each group has shared answers to questions 1 through 4 about the fender-bender role play, review with the group Handout 6–13 to ensure all content has been shared. ◆ After each group has shared answers to questions 1 through 3 about the foggy conditions demonstration/practice, review with the group Handout 6–14 to ensure that all content has been shared.	Handout 6–11: Facilitation Case Study, Handout 6–12: The Case Study, Handout 6–13: Role Play, Handout 6–14: Demonstration and Practice
10	*Conduct large group debriefing:* Ask learners if they have any questions; discuss and answer the questions.	

Handout 6–40
Structuring the Development Plan

Instructions: Identify one strength that you want to hone and two weaknesses that you want to overcome. List strengths and weaknesses in the *Areas for Development* below. Indicate with a checkmark the method(s) you plan to use in enhancing your strength or overcoming your weaknesses. An example is provided.

METHODS FOR DEVELOPMENT

AREAS FOR DEVELOPMENT	MENTOR	SEMINAR/ WORKSHOP	NETWORKING	PROFESSIONAL ORGANIZATION	INTERNSHIP	READING PROGRAM	REFLECTIVE JOURNAL	OTHER (DESCRIBE)
Example: Learning to make adjustments on the fly	√	√				√		
1.								
2.								
3.								

Instructions: For each area for development listed above, indicate your desired outcome

Desired outcome for sample area for development:

Example: To be able to make quick adjustments to the delivery of a course without sacrificing participants' learning.

Desired outcome for development area 1:

continued on next page

Handout 6–40, continued
Structuring the Development Plan

Desired outcome for development area 2:

Desired outcome for development area 3:

Instructions: For each area for development, complete the action plan below.

EXAMPLE

SPECIFIC ACTIONS TO IMPLEMENT METHOD SELECTED ABOVE	RESOURCES REQUIRED	TIMELINE	OBSTACLES	ACTIONS TO REMOVE OBSTACLES	EVIDENCE OF PROGRESS
a. *Read* Facilitation Basics	*Purchase the book*	*By June 30, 200x*	*Finding the time*	◆ *Better time management* ◆ *Make it a priority* ◆ *Have my manager hold me accountable*	*Reading two chapters per week*
b. *Receive peer coaching*	*Peers*	*August 31, 200x*	*Finding a skilled peer willing to coach me*	*Identify the peer and request the support*	*Written feedback from peer coach*

AREA FOR DEVELOPMENT 1

SPECIFIC ACTIONS TO IMPLEMENT METHOD SELECTED ABOVE	RESOURCES REQUIRED	TIMELINE	OBSTACLES	ACTIONS TO REMOVE OBSTACLES	EVIDENCE OF PROGRESS
a.					
b.					
c.					
d.					

AREA FOR DEVELOPMENT 2

SPECIFIC ACTIONS TO IMPLEMENT METHOD SELECTED ABOVE	RESOURCES REQUIRED	TIMELINE	OBSTACLES	ACTIONS TO REMOVE OBSTACLES	EVIDENCE OF PROGRESS
a.					
b.					
c.					
d.					

continued on next page

Handout 6–40, continued

Structuring the Development Plan

AREA FOR DEVELOPMENT 3

SPECIFIC ACTIONS TO IMPLEMENT METHOD SELECTED ABOVE	RESOURCES REQUIRED	TIMELINE	OBSTACLES	ACTIONS TO REMOVE OBSTACLES	EVIDENCE OF PROGRESS
a.					
b.					
c.					
d.					

Source: © 2006 Performance Advantage Group. Adapted with permission of Performance Advantage Group.

Delivery Preparation Checklist

Instructions: Here is a checklist to help you prepare to teach either the one- or two-day course on learning facilitation skills. When you complete an activity, place a checkmark (√) in the corresponding box.

ONE MONTH BEFORE THE WORKSHOP:

☐ **1.** Identify your target audience. Determine the members' average presentation skill level. Determine their average levels of facilitation knowledge and skill.

☐ **2.** Determine the audience size and tentative groupings.

☐ **3.** Schedule the training session.

☐ **4.** Design the room setup.

☐ **5.** Reserve an appropriate training room and breakout rooms; ensure the room(s) can accommodate your setup.

☐ **6.** Reserve all media, including computer projection system or overhead projector for PowerPoint slides, screen, and flipchart easels. Be sure you have one flipchart for each team and one for yourself.

☐ **7.** Make arrangements for refreshments and meals, if appropriate.

☐ **8.** Prepare copies of all participant materials, including learning activities and handouts.

☐ **9.** Begin reviewing the facilitator's materials to become familiar with the course content and flow; develop ways to make the content your own.

☐ **10.** Promote the learning event through invitation memos, letters, or emails to potential participants; encourage managers to support learners' participation. If appropriate, use flyers and posters to promote the course.

☐ **11.** Provide an easy way for learners to register; track registration.

JUST PRIOR TO THE WORKSHOP:

☐ **12.** Arrive early at the training room. Ensure that the room is set to your specifications, that needed equipment is provided, and that refreshments are there.

☐ **13.** Check that the equipment works and load your CD.

☐ **14.** Display your welcome slide.

☐ **15.** Position all flipcharts for yourself and for the group(s); ensure there are enough markers of varied colors for group work.

☐ **16.** Place masking tape, copies of all handouts and learning activities, and supplies on the materials table.

☐ **17.** Create the Parking Lot flipchart page and post it on a wall.

☐ **18.** Place a pad of sticky-notes on each table.

☐ **19.** Place one tent card at each seat and a marker on each table.

Using Media

General Tips

- Vary your media; don't use any one type of media too often. Using the same media multiple times (for example, PowerPoint presentations) is boring and repetitive.
- Choose media that are appropriate for the content and situation.
- Using varied media that will appeal to a range of learning styles and preferences throughout the course not only makes sure all learners will learn—it also builds goodwill with learners. A learner who is temporarily uncomfortable in a learning activity will tolerate it because she knows that the next activity will be more comfortable.

Flipcharts and Easels

WHEN TO USE

- At informal learning events
- To generate materials or items on the spot
- When you want to keep a visible record of work as it progresses
- When you need to keep the lights on in the training room.

TIPS

- Make your writing legible and large (six lines per page, letters two inches high).
- Keep a record of progress throughout the learning event.
- Use headings to keep your talk organized.
- Vary the colors you use. Blue and black letters are most easily seen; green and red can mean "pro" and "con" or "do" and "don't," respectively, to some learners, so use accordingly; remember, some color-blind learners can't differentiate green and red.
- Use water-based markers; they don't bleed through to the next sheet or onto the wall behind the chart.

- Leave blanks between the pages of your flipchart so the text of the next page can't be seen.
- If you're right-handed, stand to left of chart; if left-handed, stand to the right.
- Write notes to yourself in light pencil on the pages.
- Make tabs out of sticky-notes or tape so you can flip easily to the desired page.
- *Touch, turn, talk:* Write on the chart (but don't talk to the chart while writing), turn, then speak to the group.

PLUSES AND MINUSES

+ Informality creates a comfortable environment.

+ Flipcharts are good for smaller rooms.

+ Learners can make their own flipcharts to use for activities/ presentations.

+ Charts allow for good facilitator movement.

– They don't work well in large rooms; can't be seen by learners who are more than 30 feet away.

– Whoever is preparing the flipchart pages must have legible handwriting.

– They're not good for more formal groups or groups who expect a presentation supported by technology.

Overhead Transparencies

WHEN TO USE

- At informal learning events
- When generating or capturing material/ideas on the spot, using blank transparencies
- At multiple sites
- In moderate-size rooms.

TIPS

- If writing on transparencies as the workshop progresses, write legibly.
- Use multiple colors; refer to the color tips for flipcharts.
- Use large fonts and graphics.
- Clean the glass before using the overhead projector.

- To focus the projector without revealing your transparencies, place a coin with ridged edges on the glass and sharpen its projected image.

- Talk to learners, not to the glass or the screen.

- Use transparency markers.

- To draw attention to displayed items or words, point to them on the transparency positioned on the glass rather than to the projected image. Use a sharp object, such as a pen or pencil.

- Turn off the projector (a) when you've finished with the content on a transparency and you want to direct learners' attention elsewhere; and (b) when you're changing transparencies, to avoid glare.

- To reveal the content bit by bit, place a piece of paper under the transparency and slide it slowly to display one item at a time.

- As you write on a transparency, make sure that your shoulder is not blocking the projection.

PLUSES AND MINUSES

+ Learners can make their own transparencies for activities or presentations.

+ If you store, transport, and use them carefully, transparencies are great for learning events that you facilitate more than once.

+ They're easily carried with you to multiple sites.

− Using them requires fairly low room light.

− The projector may break down or the bulb may fail in the midst of your presentation.

− The keystone effect caused by the projection screen may be distracting.

− Cords can trip you and the learners.

− Too many transparencies can create a physical barrier between you and the learners because you must stand at the projector for a long time.

− Using the projector restricts your movement.

Whiteboards

WHEN TO USE

- At informal learning events
- When generating material or brainstorming items on the spot
- When you need to keep the lights on in the training room.

TIPS

- If you have enough whiteboards, keep a record of progress throughout the learning event so everyone knows where they are in the agenda.
- Make your writing legible and large (letters two inches high).
- Use headings to keep your talk organized.
- Use it to jot notes during a discussion.
- Vary the colors you use; refer to the color tips for flipcharts.
- Use dry-erase markers.
- *Touch, turn, talk:* write on the board (but don't talk to the board while writing), turn, then speak to the group.

PLUSES AND MINUSES

+ Learners can use the board for activities or presentations.

+ Whiteboards are good for smallish rooms.

− You can't move the board around the room, or take it with you to another breakout room.

− They don't work well in large rooms; can't be seen by learners who are more than 30 feet away.

− They restrict facilitator movement.

PowerPoint Slides, Digital Presentations, or Photographic Slides

WHEN TO USE

- At formal learning events
- For learning events you facilitate multiple times
- When low-tech display doesn't fit the audience's expectations.

TIPS

- Use multiple colors; for PowerPoint or photographic slides, a dark background with yellow or white lettering is best; refer to the color tips for flipcharts.
- If making handout versions of the slides, switch the color combination to black print on a white background.
- Make sure that your choice of the handout version of the slides is readable. The more print on a slide, the larger your handout version of each slide should be.

- ◆ Use large, sans serif fonts.
- ◆ Use graphics.
- ◆ Animate and build the content item by item on the screen.
- ◆ Talk to learners, not to the screen.

PLUSES AND MINUSES

+ Slides and photos can be eye-catching and very engaging.

+ These media work in large rooms with large groups, with attention to ambient lighting.

+ These presentations are easily transported on a laptop computer, or on CD, DVD, or memory chip for use where a computer and LCD projector are available already.

+ If there's a remote device for changing slides, you can move around more easily.

– Technology can break down.

– It's challenging to add display items on the fly during a learning event.

– These media require low room light.

– If there's no remote, your movement is restricted.

Videos and DVDs

WHEN TO USE

- ◆ To portray the right or wrong way to do something, for behavioral modeling

- ◆ For situational and case analysis.

TIPS

- ◆ Make sure there are enough monitors for all to see.

- ◆ Don't allow a video/film to run for a long time without breaking it up. Stop to discuss after a maximum of 15 minutes; then start up again.

- ◆ If you want to use a commercial film or excerpt from a TV program, you must seek permission from the movie studio or television network.

- ◆ Be sure settings and clothing in the film are not too dated; extraneous matters can be distracting.

PLUSES AND MINUSES

+ These are excellent ways to provide media variety.

+ They work well for content that doesn't evolve or fluctuate.

+ They work well when examining or describing skills; can show either "do" or "don't."

+ They allow for good facilitator movement.

– Film is a passive medium. Learners can become disengaged.

– Can be used for too long ("the electronic babysitter").

– Low light causes lack of attention and participation when it's used for too long.

Written Materials

WHEN TO USE

- When you want to provide reference materials for your learners

- When learners must work alone to complete a handout or self-assessment.

TIPS

- Use colors and graphics; refer to the tips for flipcharts.

- Provide white space for note taking.

- Leave blanks for structured note taking.

- Hand them out as they are needed so learners don't read ahead.

- Handouts for use in class should contain bullet points with lots of white space. Text-heavy handouts should be used for later reference.

- PowerPoint and digital presentations can be printed as handouts and distributed for later reference.

- On occasion, have learners read segments aloud during discussion. This helps engage auditory learners.

PLUSES AND MINUSES

+ They give more detailed information for later reference.

+ They're great for visual learners.

+ The structured note-taking version of a handout is great for kinesthetic learners.

– They don't "resonate" with auditory learners.

Props and Objects

WHEN TO USE

- ◆ When you want to make a point especially memorable.

TIPS

- ◆ Use your imagination in selecting props and objects; be creative and take advantage of your own special talent.
- ◆ Choose props that are natural and comfortable for you.
- ◆ Make sure the analogy you're drawing by using the prop to illustrate a point is accurate and easily understood.

PLUSES AND MINUSES

+ Can be memorable and make your point more vibrant.

+ Can bring fun into the workshop.

– Props may not be very portable.

– How they are understood and received by participants may depend on learners' frames of reference and experience.

Source: Adapted with permission from Deborah Davis Tobey and Deb Tobey LLC, 2003.

Using the Compact Disc

Insert the CD and locate the file *How to Use This CD.doc.*

Contents of the CD

The compact disc that accompanies this workbook on training in facilitation contains three types of files. All of the files can be used on a variety of computer platforms.

- **Adobe .pdf documents.** These include handouts, checklists, evaluations, and exhibits.

- **Microsoft PowerPoint presentations.** These presentations add interest and depth to many of the training activities included in the workbook.

- **Microsoft PowerPoint files for overhead transparency masters.** These files make it easy to print viewgraphs and handouts in black-and-white rather than using an office copier. They contain only text and line drawings; there are no images to print in grayscale.

Computer Requirements

To read or print the .pdf files on the CD, you must have Adobe Acrobat Reader software installed on your system. The program can be downloaded at no cost from the Adobe website, www.adobe.com.

To use or adapt the contents of the PowerPoint presentation files on the CD, you must have Microsoft PowerPoint software installed on your computer. If you simply want to view the PowerPoint documents, you must have an appropriate viewer installed on your computer. Microsoft provides various viewers free for downloading from its website, www.microsoft.com.

Printing from the CD

TEXT FILES

You can print the training materials using Adobe Acrobat Reader. Simply open the .pdf file and print as many copies as you need. The following .pdf documents can be directly printed from the CD:

- Exhibit 2–1: Facilitator Behavioral Competencies
- Handout 6–1: Presenter and Facilitator: What's the Difference?
- Handout 6–2: Facilitator Self-Assessment
- Handout 6–3: Factors for Room Setup
- Handout 6–4: Aligning Learning Activities and Media with Learning Preferences
- Handout 6–5: Learning Styles
- Handout 6–6: Recognizing Learning Styles
- Handout 6–7: Aligning Learning Activities with Learning Preferences and Styles
- Handout 6–8: The Interactive Lecture
- Handout 6–9: The Guided Discussion
- Handout 6–10: The Structured Bridge Activity
- Handout 6–11: Facilitation Case Study
- Handout 6–12: The Case Study
- Handout 6–13: The Role Play
- Handout 6–14: The Demonstration and Practice
- Handout 6–15: Behavioral Checklist for a Structured Bridge Activity
- Handout 6–16: Behavioral Checklist for a Guided Discussion
- Handout 6–17: Setting Up Instructions and Monitoring Learning Activities (Partial)
- Handout 6–18: Grouping Learners in Learning Activities (Partial)
- Handout 6–19: Sequencing Learning Activities and Giving Feedback (Partial)
- Handout 6–20: Using Media (Partial)
- Handout 6–21: Physical Presentation Tips (Partial)
- Handout 6–22: Setting Up Instructions and Monitoring Learning Activities (Complete)
- Handout 6–23: Grouping Learners in Learning Activities (Complete)

- Handout 6–24: Sequencing Learning Activities and Giving Feedback (Complete)
- Handout 6–25: Using Media (Complete)
- Handout 6–26: Physical Presentation Tips (Complete)
- Handout 6–27: Checklist for Room Setup
- Handout 6–28: Sample Room Layouts
- Handout 6–29: Room Setup Considerations
- Handout 6–30: Tips for Room Setup
- Handout 6–31: Strategies for Dealing with Disruptive Behavior
- Handout 6–32: Recognizing and Responding to Disruptive Learner Behavior
- Handout 6–33: Recommended Strategies to Deal with Disruptive Behaviors
- Handout 6–34: A Comprehensive Response for Dealing with Disruptive Behaviors
- Handout 6–35: Factors in Adjusting on the Fly
- Handout 6–36: Sample Module Plan—Creating the Climate and Environment for Learning
- Handout 6–37: Advanced Facilitation Skills Training Course Evaluation
- Handout 6–38: Facilitation Skills Training Course Evaluation
- Handout 6–39: Sample Module Plan—Skill Practices Case Study
- Handout 6–40: Structuring the Development Plan
- Development Plan Worksheet
- Facilitation Guidelines
- Media Checklist

POWERPOINT SLIDES

You may print the presentation slides directly from this CD using Microsoft PowerPoint. Simply open the .ppt files and print as many copies as you need. You also may make handouts of the presentations by printing two, four, or six slides per page. These slides will be in color, with design elements embedded. PowerPoint also permits you to print these in grayscale or black-and-white, although printing from the overhead masters files will yield better black-and-white representations. Many trainers who use laptop computers to project their presentations bring along viewgraphs just in case there are glitches in the system. The overhead masters can be printed from the PowerPoint .pps files.

Table C–1

Navigating Through a PowerPoint Presentation

KEY	POWERPOINT "SHOW" ACTION
Space bar *or* Enter *or* Mouse click	Advance through custom animations embedded in the presentation
Backspace	Back up to the last projected element of the presentation
Escape	Abort the presentation
B *or* b	Blank the screen to black
B *or* b *(repeat)*	Resume the presentation
W *or* w	Blank the screen to white
W *or* w *(repeat)*	Resume the presentation

Adapting the PowerPoint Slides

You can modify or otherwise customize the slides by opening and editing them in the appropriate application. However, you must display the original source of the material—it is illegal to pass it off as your own work. You may indicate that a document was adapted from this workbook, copyrighted by ASTD. The files will open as "Read Only," so before you adapt them you will need to save them onto your hard drive under a different file name.

Showing the PowerPoint Presentations

On the CD, the following PowerPoint presentations are included:

- ◆ *One-day.ppt*
- ◆ *Two-day.ppt*
- ◆ *One-day.pps*
- ◆ *Two-day.pps*

Having the presentations in .ppt format means that they automatically show full-screen when you double-click on a file name. You also can open the Microsoft PowerPoint application and launch the presentations from there.

Use the space bar, the enter key, or mouse clicks to advance through a show. Press the backspace key to back up. Use the escape key to abort a presentation. If you want to blank the screen to black while the group discusses a point, press the B key. Pressing it again restores the show. If you want to blank the screen to a white background, do the same with the W key. Table C–1 summarizes these instructions.

We strongly recommend that trainers practice making presentations with the PowerPoint slides before using them in live training situations. You should be confident that you can cogently expand on the points featured in the presentations and discuss the methods for working through them. If you want to engage your training participants fully (rather than worrying about how to show the next slide), become familiar with this simple technology before you need to use it. A good practice is to insert notes into the *Speaker's Notes* feature of the PowerPoint program, print them out, and have them in front of you when you present the slides.

For Further Reading

ADULT LEARNING

Merriam, S., ed. 2001. *New Directions for Adult and Continuing Education.* San Francisco: Jossey-Bass.

Merriam, S. B., and R. S. Cafarella. 1998. *Learning in Adulthood: A Comprehensive Guide.* San Francisco: Jossey-Bass.

Swanson, R. A. 1998. *The Adult Learner: The Definitive Classic In Adult Education and Human Resource Development,* 5th ed. Houston: Gulf.

Vella, J. 2002. *Learning to Listen, Learning to Teach: The Power of Dialogue in Educating Adults.* San Francisco: Jossey-Bass.

FACILITATOR COMPETENCIES AND FACILITATION SKILLS

Eitington, J. E. 1989. *The Winning Trainer,* 2nd ed. Houston: Gulf.

Hunter, D., A. Bailey, and B. Taylor. 1995. *The Art of Facilitation.* Tucson, AZ: Fisher Books.

Justice, T., and D. W. Jamieson. 1999. *The Facilitator's Fieldbook.* New York: AMACOM.

Kearny, L. 1995. *The Facilitator's Toolkit: Tools and Techniques for Generating Ideas and Making Decisions in Groups.* Amherst, MA: HRD Press.

Kinlaw, D. 1996. *The ASTD Trainers Sourcebook: Facilitation Skills.* New York: McGraw-Hill.

McCain, D., and D. Tobey. 2004. *Facilitation Basics.* Alexandria, VA: ASTD Press.

Rumsey, T. A. 1996. *Not Just Games: Strategic Uses of Experiential Learning to Drive Business Results.* Dubuque, IA: Kendall-Hunt.

Shapiro, L. T. 1995. *Training Effectiveness Handbook: A High-Results System for Design, Delivery, and Evaluation.* New York: McGraw-Hill.

Wheelan, S. A. 1990. *Facilitating Training Groups: A Guide to Leadership and Verbal Intervention Skills.* New York: Praeger.

PRESENTATION SKILLS

Becker, D., and P. B. Becker. 1994. *Powerful Presentation Skills.* Chicago: Irwin Professional Publishing/McGraw-Hill.

Burn, B. E. 1996. *Flip Chart Power: Secrets of the Masters.* San Diego, CA: Pfeiffer.

Jolles, R. L. 2000. *How to Run Seminars and Workshops: Presentation Skills for Consultants, Trainers, and Teachers.* New York: John Wiley & Sons.

Peoples, D. A. 1997. *Presentations Plus: David Peoples' Proven Techniques,* rev. ed. New York: John Wiley & Sons.

Pike, R., and D. Arch. 1997. *Dealing With Difficult Participants: 127 Practical Strategies for Minimizing Resistance and Maximizing Results in Your Presentations.* San Francisco: Jossey-Bass/Pfeiffer.

Rosania, R. 2003. *Presentation Basics.* Alexandria, VA: ASTD Press.

Silberman, M., and K. Clark. 1999. *101 Ways to Make Meetings Active: Surefire Ideas to Engage Your Group.* San Diego, CA: Pfeiffer.

Stettner, M. 2002. *Mastering Business Presentations.* McLean, VA: National Institute of Business Management.

Zelazny, G. 1999. *Say It With Presentations: How to Design and Deliver Successful Business Presentations.* New York: McGraw-Hill.

INSTRUCTIONAL DEVELOPMENT AND LEARNING ACTIVITY DEVELOPMENT

Anglin, G. 1991. *Instructional Technology: Past, Present and Future.* Englewood, CO: Libraries Unlimited.

Barca, M., and K. Cobb. 1996. *Beginnings & Endings: Creative Warmups & Closure Activities.* Amherst, MA: HRD Press.

Clark, R. 1989. *Developing Technical Training: A Structured Approach for the Development of Classroom and Computer-Based Instructional Materials.* Reading, MA: Addison-Wesley.

Hattori, R. A., and J. Wycoff. 2004. *Innovation Training.* Alexandria, VA: ASTD Press.

Hodell, C. 2006. *ISD From the Ground Up: A No-Nonsense Approach to Instructional Design.* Alexandria, VA: ASTD Press.

Jones, K. 1997. *Creative Events for Trainers.* New York: McGraw-Hill.

Nadler, L. 1989. *Designing Training Programs: The Critical Events Model.* Reading, MA: Addison-Wesley.

Nadler, L., and Z. Nadler. 1994. *Designing Training Programs: The Critical Events Model,* 2nd ed. Houston: Gulf.

Newstron, J. W., and E. E. Scannell. 1994. *Even More Games Trainers Play.* New York: McGraw-Hill.

Pfeiffer, J. W., and J. E. Jones. 1976–present. *The Annual Handbook for Group Facilitators.* New York: John Wiley & Sons.

Silberman, M. 1990. *Active Training: Handbook of Techniques, Designs, Case Examples, and Tips.* New York: Lexington Books.

Silberman, M., and K. Lawson. 1995. *101 Ways to Make Training Active.* San Diego, CA: Pfeiffer.

MEASUREMENT AND EVALUATION

Bassi, L. *What Works: Assessment, Development, and Measurement.* Alexandria, VA: ASTD Press.

Broad, M. 1997. *In Action: Transferring Learning to the Workplace.* Alexandria, VA: ASTD Press.

Combs, W. L., and S. V. Falletta. 2000. *The Targeted Evaluation Process.* Alexandria, VA: ASTD Press.

Horton, W. 2001. *Evaluating E-Learning.* Alexandria, VA: ASTD Press.

Kirkpatrick, D. 1994. *Evaluating Training Programs: The Four Levels.* San Francisco: Berrett-Koehler.

McCain, D. 2005. *Evaluation Basics.* Alexandria, VA: ASTD Press.

Parry, S. 2004. *Evaluating the Impact of Training.* Alexandria, VA: ASTD Press.

Phillips, J. 1994. *In Action: Measuring Return on Investment.* Alexandria, VA: ASTD Press.

Phillips, J., Phillips, P. P., and T. K. Hodges. 2004. *Make Training Evaluation Work.* Alexandria, VA: ASTD Press.

Stadius, R., ed. 1999. *More Evaluation Instruments: ASTD Trainer's Toolkit.* Alexandria, VA: ASTD Press.

Swanson, R. A., and E. Holton. 1999. *Results: How to Assess Performance, Learning, and Perceptions in Organizations.* San Francisco: Berrett-Koehler.

NEEDS ANALYSIS

Mager, R. F., and P. Pipe. 1989. *Analyzing Performance Problems.* Belmont, CA: Pittman Learning.

Phillips, J., and E. F. Holton. 1995. *In Action: Conducting Needs Assessment.* Alexandria, VA: ASTD Press.

Swanson, R. 1996. *Analysis for Improving Performance.* San Francisco: Berrett-Koehler.

Tobey, D. 2005. *Needs Assessment Basics.* Alexandria, VA: ASTD Press.

GENERAL HRD MATERIAL

Charney, C., and K. Conway. 2004. *The Trainer's Tool Kit,* 2nd ed. New York: AMACOM.

Craig, R. 1987. *Training and Development Handbook,* 3rd ed. New York: McGraw-Hill.

Mitchell, G. 1998. *The Trainer's Handbook: The AMA Guide to Effective Training,* 3rd ed. New York: AMACOM.

Rosenbaum, S., and J. Williams. 2004. *Learning Paths: Increase Profits by Reducing the Time It Takes Employees to Get Up-to-Speed.* San Francisco: Pfeiffer.

Donald V. McCain is founder and principal of Performance Advantage Group, an organization dedicated to helping companies gain competitive advantage through the development of their human resources. With years of corporate and consulting experience, McCain's focus is on design and development of custom learning experiences in leadership, sales and marketing, call center management, and many areas of professional development that result in improved business unit and individual performance. He also consults in HRD processes, including design/development, competency identification and development, certification, evaluation (including transfer and return-on-investment), presentation and facilitation, and managing and marketing the HRD function. Most of his clients are *Fortune* 100 companies across various industries. His work is international in scope. McCain also has advised many new consultants on the business side of training consulting.

McCain has a bachelor's degree in business administration, a master's degree of divinity, a master's degree in business administration with a concentration in HR and marketing, and a doctorate in education in HRD from Vanderbilt University, Nashville, TN. He is a member of the Society for Human Resource Management and the Academy of Human Resource Development. In addition, McCain is a visiting professor at the School of Business at Tennessee State University and a former adjunct professor for the School of Management at Belmont University, Nashville. McCain also teaches for the University of Phoenix. He served previously as an adjunct assistant professor of leadership and organizations for Vanderbilt University.

McCain is the author of the ASTD Press publications *Creating Training Courses (When You're Not a Trainer)* (1999) and *Evaluation Basics* (2005); and, with Deb

Tobey, he co-authored *Facilitation Basics* (2004). Additionally, he has published several articles and evaluation instruments.

McCain lives in Nashville, with his wife Kathy and their two boys, Weston and Colin. He also has two married daughters, Kimberly and Karla. McCain may be contacted at *donpag@bellsouth.net.*

Building on her 20 years' experience in the field, **Deborah Davis Tobey** is fortunate to function concurrently in both internal and external consultant roles. She is vice president of organization development at Comdata Corporation, an innovative transaction and payment-processing company headquartered in Brentwood, TN; and she is principal of Deb Tobey LLC, a consulting practice in human and organization performance improvement. She works with client organizations in consulting skills development and consulting systems; training needs assessment, design, facilitation, and evaluation; train-the-trainer programs; strategic planning; teambuilding; group process consultation; competency modeling; and leadership development. Tobey's clients include *Fortune* 500 organizations in manufacturing, finance, importing, health care, the service sector; and nonprofit organizations, state and local governments, and universities. She often operates in a mentoring/coaching role with HRD professionals and students, and has served ASTD in several officer capacities for 10 years.

Tobey has a bachelor's degree in English and a master's degree in student personnel administration and counseling from Virginia Tech, Blacksburg, VA. Her doctorate in HRD is from Vanderbilt University, Nashville, TN. She served for four years as adjunct professor of the practice in human resource development at Vanderbilt, and is an adjunct professor in the HRD graduate program at George Washington University, Washington, DC. She has authored or co-authored three other books published by ASTD Press: *Facilitation Basics* (2005), *Needs Assessment Basics* (2006), and *Data Collection for Needs Assessment* (*Infoline* 2007).

She lives in Nashville with her husband Bryan Tobey, and may be reached at *dtobey@mindspring.com* or *www.debtobey.com.*

◆